·THE·

COBBLER
CRUSADE

MAIN COURSES AND DESSERTS

Bringing an Old-Fashioned
Dish to Modern Cooks

by Irene Ritter

FISHER
BOOKS

Publishers	Bill Fisher
	Helen Fisher
	Howard Fisher
Editor	Veronica Durie
Art Director	David Fischer
Book Production	Casa Cold Type, Inc.
Published by	Fisher Books
	4239 W. Ina Road
	Tucson, AZ 85741
	(602) 744-6110

© 1992 Fisher Books
Printed in U.S.A.
Printing 10 9 8 7 6 5 4

**Library of Congress
Cataloging-in-Publication Data**

Ritter, Irene S.
    The Cobbler Crusade: bringing
an old-fashioned dish to modern cooks/
by Irene S. Ritter
      p. cm.
    Includes index
    ISBN 1-55561-044-7: $9.95
    1. Desserts. 2. Cookery (Fruit).
    I. Title
TX773.R59 1992   92-12019
641.8'652—dc20   CIP

Table of Contents

About the Author

Irene Ritter, a Chicago native and alumna of Loyola University's Lake Shore campus, now shares an isolated mountain retreat in Oregon's scenic Columbia Gorge with her husband and two Siamese cats.

For 14 years, Irene has worked as a Portland freelance journalist, public-relations consultant and graphic artist. Her food and lifestyle stories have appeared in *The Oregonian, Country Woman* and other national publications.

A tradition of baking has been shared in her mother's family for generations, starting with her great-grandfather, Franco Conti, who established bakeries throughout Sicily in the late 19th century.

Dedication

Dedicated to Bill Gore, Sr., Pasadena's Cobbler King who preaches delicious things about time, love and peach cobblers.

Acknowledgments

The author wishes to acknowledge the creative assistance of the following people: Merle Alexander, assistant editor of *FOODday/The Oregonian* in Portland, Oregon; Jim Nelson; Margaret Doti; the Thompson Mill testers; and Jeff Ritter.

All About Cobblers

What is a Cobbler?

New Englanders sometimes refer to them as grunts or slumps. But most people know them as cobblers. Not only are there different names for this all-American dessert, cooks also argue about what truly makes a cobbler a cobbler.

One battle among cobbler lovers rages over crust. Should crusts be made of biscuit, pastry, crumbled cookie dough or cake batter? Should they line the bottoms or tops of fruit; or be latticed or shaped like cobblestones? There's even more confusion over shape. Should cobblers be rectangular or round?

And how do you define cobbler when there are so many variations?

Instead of coming up with a clear-cut definition of a cobbler, I would like to challenge cooks to make up a few of their own. Let's start by expanding the notion of cobblers to include savory brunch and dinner options. Thus, a variety of ingredients may be introduced into a basic biscuit recipe—like nuts, coconut and cream cheese for dessert crusts; or herbs, cheeses, sour cream, chopped onions, poppy seeds and rye flour for brunch or dinner crusts.

Though we're breathing new life into cobblers, we can't ignore a cobbler's humble beginnings as a Colonial-American breakfast dish. So, in step with the early settlers' virtues of practical home economics, many of the recipes are quick and easy to prepare with fresh ingredients.

This does not imply, however, that cobbler dining should be hurried. Cobblers are in the category of those cozy homemade dishes meant to be eaten slowly, lingered over—perhaps with coffee, espresso or tea; a complementary wine; a warm fire; and plenty of conversation among guests and friends.

How Cobblers Were Named

Some food experts claim a shoe-cobbler's wife created the dish, while others suggest a cobbler may once have been a tall, iced drink of wine, rum or whiskey and sugar. To date, the most plausible answer is that cobblers were named after cobblestones. Picture a fruit, meat or vegetable filling covered with mounds of crust. Doesn't it bring to mind a cobblestone alley straight out of a medieval fairy tale?

Cobbler Crusts

As for cobbler dough, there are two schools of thought. Many chefs consider pastry or pie crust—made without baking powder—to be true cobbler crust. Though, there's nothing wrong with good pastry dough, *The Cobbler Crusade* adheres to the more traditional practice of beginning with a basic biscuit crust. Then a host of other ingredients can be added to complement or vary textures.

For example, eggs tend to turn dough a bit like batter, yielding a cake-like consistency to the biscuit. Baking with brown sugar strongly signals the aroma and flavor of molasses. Granulated sugar, cornmeal and chopped pecans create crunchy textures. Combining white and whole-wheat flours or rolled oats and raisins renders a substantial, hearty crust; while heavy creams, sour cream and buttermilk are best for buttery, shortcake biscuits.

Cobbler Dough

Shortcut Method

If time is a factor in your cooking, you'll welcome my fast-and-easy method for blending the biscuit crust's ingredients.

- Start by mixing the dry ingredients like flour, baking powder and sugar, then pouring in butter or margarine melted on the stovetop or in a microwave oven. Pouring cooled melted butter or margarine into dry ingredients sacrifices a bit of flaky-biscuit perfection, but certainly not enough to worry about additional preliminary steps.

- Next, add the cream or milk and stir all the ingredients together with a wooden spoon or fork. But, don't stir too much—not for more than 30 seconds—or your dough will become too sticky. My recipe steps are designed for people who don't have the time or inclination at the end of a long day to use the French pastry chef's method of cutting butter into dry ingredients. And, I've even saved time over the practice of scooping a hollow in the middle of the ingredients and then filling the hole with milk or cream.

Traditional Method

Many cooks regard these steps to be as ritualistic as brewing a morning cup of coffee, espresso or tea. So, if you're hesitant about breaking tradition, here are steps sanctioned by blue-ribbon biscuit makers.

- Use your thumbs and fingertips, a pastry blender or two knives cutting against each other to distribute cold butter through the dry ingredients. (Even your fingertips should be cold.) The end result should be a slightly crumbly texture.

• Dig a well in the center for adding cold cream, milk or other liquids. Next comes a few quick turns of a wooden spoon or fork—but not for more than 30 seconds or you'll increase the chances for a tougher crust and reduce the odds for easy rolling.

To Roll Dough

• After the butter or margarine is cut into dry ingredients and liquid added, form a ball of dough and place on a lightly floured surface.

• Marble is the best rolling surface because it keeps the butter and liquid ingredients cool. Or, you can use a pastry cloth or wooden board as a rolling surface.

• Flatten the center of the dough with a rolling pin. Using even pressure, roll the pin away from you to the edge; never roll back and forth.

• Keep rolling from the center of the dough out to the edge until the dough is 1/8 inch thick.

Cobbler Creams and Milk

The richer the milk solids, the flakier the biscuit. The majority of shortcake biscuit cobblers are made with whipping cream. Most warm-fruit cobblers are best served with whipped cream or a jug of cream. Other milk products include: half and half, whole milk, lowfat and skim milk.

Cobbler Shortening

Butter is the recommended shortening, simply because of the rich taste it lends to biscuit and pastry dough.

However, feel free to experiment with margarine made with canola oils, which is the shortening of choice in my lowered saturated-fat chapter, Lower Fat Cobblers.

Cobbler Sugars

All crust and fruit recipes featured in the dessert sections call for added sugars but in lowered amounts when compared to many other cookbook suggestions. Reducing sugar allows the flavor of the fruit to be enhanced rather than overpowered by sweetness. Many recipes suggest brown sugar, instead of white, refined sugar. Brown sugar is either white sugar colored with molasses or burnt white sugar. Try the molasses variety, for it adds color to crusts and turns cobblers into sweet-smelling sensations. Moreover, the added molasses contains some essential minerals, calcium and iron.

Bare Utensils

Cobbler utensils are simple, requiring minimal cleanup. For mixing ingredients, the essentials include a wooden spoon or fork and large and medium-size bowls. A fork or handheld electric mixer are ideal for mixing crunchy cookie crusts.

As for baking equipment, most recipes call for 8-, 9- or 10-inch baking pans or dishes (with sides about 1-1/2 inches high). A few crowd-sized cobblers are baked in 13" x 9" pans. The deep sides of pans or dishes stop fruit fillings from leaking out of pans into warm ovens. Use metal, pyrex or ceramic dishes.

Baking Powder

Always use double-acting baking powder.

About Food Processors

As with a handheld electric mixer, a food processor is great for mixing crunchy or crumbly cookie crusts, but not recommended for biscuit dough unless you use very cold butter or margarine. If you use butter or margarine at room temperature, your dough becomes overworked and too sticky.

Food Processing Biscuit or Shortcake Dough

- Make certain butter or margarine is chilled for easy blending. Process the dry ingredients with chilled butter or margarine until the mixture turns coarse and crumbly in texture.

- While the processor is running, pour milk, cream or other liquids down the tube until the dough begins to form.

- Simply spoon dough over fruit or other fillings.

Food Processor Crisp Crusts

- Cream the chilled butter or margarine, sugar and liquids until smooth—about one minute. Stop the motor once to scrape the sides of the bowl; then slowly spoon in the flour and other dry ingredients until the mixture is evenly blended.

- Using your thumbs and fingertips, crumble dough on top of fillings.

Note: In most of my recipes, the butter is pre-melted and mixed in with a wooden spoon. If you use a food processor, do not use warm or melted butter.

Reduced Fat

Recognizing the fact that many people are concerned about reducing fat in their diets, where appropriate, I offer the option of using butter or margarine, or 2% lowfat milk in place of cream.

Dessert Cobblers

By varying the amounts of butter, cream, sugar and spices, you can create a host of dessert crusts. There are shortcake biscuits, crisp cobblers, crusts with lowered saturated fats, crunchy cookie crusts and cake cobblers. Within these categories are even more options. For example, the most basic short-cake biscuit is featured with a basic peach filling, while the most lusciously rich is the cream-cheese-and-pecan combination covering a cherry-and-kirsch filling.

Dessert creams and custards go well with crunchy cookie crusts, while cornmeal is a sure bet for warm cranberry. But, most crusts can be interchanged with any warm fruit filling. The sky's the limit on versatility. So freely experiment by mixing and matching.

Shortcake-Biscuit Cobblers

Biscuits made with heavier creams, butter or cream cheese almost cross the fine line into becoming shortbread. But because of their baking powder, they never quite make it over, so we're calling them shortcake biscuits. Deliciously buttery and flaky, they're not intended for calorie counters.

Peach Cobbler

You can't go wrong with the peach cobbler, especially when it has a rich and buttery shortcake biscuit. Try matching this versatile crust with any warm fruit filling.

Peach Filling:

**8 to 10 ripe peaches or 5-1/4 cups
    sliced canned Elberta peaches, drained**
3 tablespoons granulated sugar
1-1/2 tablespoons quick-cooking tapioca
2 teaspoons vanilla extract
2 tablespoons melted butter or margarine

Preheat oven to 425F (220C). Grease an 8-inch-square baking pan or dish.

Before peeling, drop fresh peaches into very hot water about 1 minute. Peel and halve peaches, remove pits and cut flesh into sixths. In a large mixing bowl, carefully spoon together peaches, sugar, tapioca and vanilla. Pour peach filling into greased baking pan or dish; drizzle melted butter or margarine on top and set aside.

Basic Shortcake Crust:

1-1/2 cups all-purpose flour
2 teaspoons baking powder
1/4 cup packed brown sugar
1/4 cup melted butter or margarine (4 tablespoons)
1/2 cup whipping cream or 2% lowfat milk

Vanilla ice cream, whipped cream or cream

In another large bowl, combine crust ingredients. Stir vigorously with a wooden spoon about 30 seconds until a stiff dough forms. Spoon dough on top of peaches to create a cobblestone effect. Bake 20 to 25 minutes or until crust is golden brown. Cool 30 minutes; then serve with vanilla ice cream, whipped cream or a jug of cream. Makes 5 or 6 servings.

Cherry-Cream-Cheese Cobbler

This recipe calls for red pie cherries enhanced with a little kirsch and topped with a shortcake biscuit featuring cream cheese and chopped pecans.

Cherry Filling:

5-1/4 cups canned, pitted, red, pie cherries, drained (about 2-1/2 lbs.)
1/3 cup cherry juice from can
1/4 cup packed brown sugar
2 tablespoons quick-cooking tapioca
2 tablespoons kirsch
1-1/2 tablespoons melted butter or margarine

Preheat oven to 425F (220C). Grease an 8-inch-square baking pan or dish.

In a large mixing bowl, carefully spoon together cherries, juice, brown sugar, tapioca and kirsch. Pour cherry filling into greased baking pan or dish; drizzle melted butter or margarine on top and set aside.

Cream-Cheese Shortcake Crust:

1-1/2 cups all-purpose flour
2 teaspoons baking powder
3-1/2 tablespoons granulated sugar
3/4 (3-oz.) pkg. cream cheese, softened
1/4 cup melted butter or margarine (4 tablespoons)
3/4 cup whole milk or 2% lowfat milk
Whipped cream flavored with kirsch

In another large bowl, combine crust ingredients. Stir vigorously with a wooden spoon about 30 seconds until a stiff dough forms. Spoon cream-cheese dough on top of cherry-kirsch filling to create a cobblestone effect. Bake 20 to 25 minutes or until crust is golden brown. Cool 30 minutes; then serve with kirsch-flavored whipped cream. Makes 5 or 6 servings.

Apple-Pecan Cobbler

*Crunchy apples and a pecan crust topped with a vanilla
glaze conjure up a sublime vision for apple lovers.
Best apples to use include: Gravenstein, Granny Smith,
Pippin, Rome Beauty and Winesap.*

Apple Filling:

4 to 6 apples, peeled and sliced (5-1/4 cups)
3 tablespoons brown sugar
1 tablespoon honey
1-1/2 tablespoons quick-cooking tapioca
1 tablespoon lemon juice
1/2 teaspoon ground cinnamon
1/4 cup chopped pecans
1-1/2 tablespoons melted butter or margarine

Preheat oven to 425F (220C). Grease an 8-inch-square
baking pan or dish.

In a large mixing bowl, carefully spoon together apples,
brown sugar, honey, tapioca, lemon juice, cinnamon and
chopped pecans. Pour apple filling into greased baking
pan or dish; drizzle melted butter or margarine on top
and set aside.

Pecan Shortcake Crust:

1-1/2 cups all-purpose flour
2 teaspoons baking powder
1/4 cup granulated sugar
1/2 cup chopped pecans
1/4 cup melted butter or margarine (4 tablespoons)
1/2 cup whipping cream or 2% lowfat milk

In another large bowl, combine crust ingredients. Stir vigorously with a wooden spoon about 30 seconds until a stiff dough forms. Spoon pecan dough on top of apple-pecan filling to create a cobblestone effect. Bake 20 to 25 minutes or until crust is golden brown. Cool 15 minutes before adding glaze.

Vanilla Glaze:

1-1/3 cups powdered sugar
1/4 cup whole milk or 2% lowfat milk
1/4 cup melted butter or margarine (4 tablespoons)
1 teaspoon vanilla extract

While cobbler is cooling, prepare glaze. In a medium saucepan, stir powdered sugar and milk over low to medium heat until smooth, 3 to 4 minutes. Remove from heat; stir in butter or margarine and vanilla. Set aside to cool about 5 minutes; then pour over cooled cobbler to form glaze. Serve immediately. Makes 5 or 6 servings.

Bing-Cherry Cobbler

Enjoy the outstanding flavor of fresh Bing cherries paired with a delicious sour-cream crust.

Bing-Cherry Filling:

5-1/4 cups pitted Bing cherries (about 2 lbs.)
2 tablespoons brown sugar
1 tablespoon honey
2 tablespoons quick-cooking tapioca
1/3 cup apple juice
1 teaspoon vanilla extract
1-1/2 tablespoons melted butter or margarine

Preheat oven to 425F (220C). Grease an 8-inch-square baking pan or dish.

In a large mixing bowl, carefully spoon together cherries, brown sugar, honey, tapioca, apple juice and vanilla. Pour cherry filling into greased baking pan or dish; drizzle melted butter or margarine on top and set aside.

Sour-Cream Shortcake Crust:

1-1/3 cups all-purpose flour
2 teaspoons baking powder
3-1/2 tablespoons granulated sugar
1/4 cup melted butter or margarine (4 tablespoons)
1/2 cup dairy sour cream

Whipped cream topped with fresh Bing cherries

In another large bowl, combine crust ingredients. Stir vigorously with a wooden spoon about 30 seconds until a stiff dough forms. Spoon sour-cream dough on top of cherry filling to create a cobblestone effect. Bake 20 to 25 minutes or until crust is golden brown. Cool 30 minutes; then serve with whipped cream garnished with Bing cherries. Makes 5 or 6 servings.

Bubbling Blackberry Cobbler

When blackberries are in season and are combined with a delicious brown-sugar shortcake crust, the end result is a glimpse of blackberry heaven.

Blackberry Filling:

5-1/4 cups fresh or slightly thawed frozen blackberries
1/4 cup granulated sugar
2 tablespoons quick-cooking tapioca
3 tablespoons lemon juice
  (juice of 1 medium-sized lemon)
1-1/2 tablespoons melted butter or margarine

Preheat oven to 425F (220C). Grease an 8-inch-square baking pan or dish.

Wash fresh blackberries thoroughly. In a large mixing bowl, carefully spoon together blackberries, sugar, tapioca and lemon juice. Pour blackberry filling into greased baking pan or dish; drizzle melted butter or margarine on top and set aside.

Brown-Sugar Shortcake Crust:

1-1/2 cups all-purpose flour
2 teaspoons baking powder
1/4 cup packed brown sugar
1/4 cup melted butter or margarine (4 tablespoons)
1/2 cup whipping cream or 2% lowfat milk

Vanilla ice cream, whipped cream or cream

In another large bowl, combine crust ingredients. Stir vigorously with a wooden spoon about 30 seconds until a stiff dough forms. Spoon dough on top of blackberries to create a cobblestone effect. Bake 20 to 25 minutes or until crust is golden brown. Cool 30 minutes; then serve with vanilla ice cream, whipped cream or a jug of cream. Makes 5 or 6 servings.

Raisin-Pecan Cobbler

Perhaps the best time to enjoy this rich all-season cobbler is during a late winter afternoon tea. The crust features oats and lemon zest.

Raisin-Pecan Filling:

3 cups (loose) seedless black raisins (1 lb.)
2 cups water
1/4 cup granulated sugar
3 tablespoons butter or margarine
2 tablespoons all-purpose flour
2 egg yolks, well-beaten
1/4 cup chopped pecans
3 tablespoons lemon juice
**   (juice of 1 medium-sized lemon)**

Preheat oven to 425F (220C). Lightly grease an 8-inch-square baking pan or dish.

In a large saucepan, heat raisins and water to boiling. Reduce heat to medium and cook 5 minutes, stirring frequently. Gradually stir in remaining ingredients, stirring 5 minutes or until mixture thickens. Pour into lightly greased baking pan or dish and set aside.

Lemon-Oat Shortcake Crust:

1 cup all-purpose flour
1/2 cup quick rolled oats
2 teaspoons baking powder
1/4 cup granulated sugar
1 tablespoon grated lemon zest
1/4 cup melted butter or margarine (4 tablespoons)
1/3 cup whipping cream or 2% lowfat milk
Vanilla ice cream, whipped cream or cream

In a large bowl, combine crust ingredients. Stir vigorously with a wooden spoon about 30 seconds until a stiff dough forms. Spoon dough on top of raisin-pecan filling to create a cobblestone effect. Bake 20 to 25 minutes or until crust is golden brown. Cool 30 minutes; then serve with vanilla ice cream, whipped cream or a jug of cream. Makes 6 or 7 servings.

Apricot Cobbler

For best results, select very ripe apricots. This cobbler features a buttery shortcake crust and an almond-cream topping.

Apricot Filling:

5-1/2 cups sliced apricots (about 2 lbs.)
1/3 cup granulated sugar
2 tablespoons quick-cooking tapioca
1/4 teaspoon almond extract
2 tablespoons melted butter or margarine

Preheat oven to 425F (220C). Grease a 9-inch-square baking pan or dish.

In a large mixing bowl, carefully spoon together apricots, sugar, tapioca and almond extract. Pour apricot filling into greased baking pan or dish; drizzle melted butter or margarine on top and set aside.

Shortcake Crust:

1-1/2 cups all-purpose flour
2 teaspoons baking powder
1/4 cup granulated sugar
1/4 cup melted butter or margarine (4 tablespoons)
1/2 cup whipping cream or 2% lowfat milk

Topping:

Whipped cream blended with slivered almonds

In another large bowl, combine crust ingredients. Stir vigorously with a wooden spoon until a stiff dough forms. Spoon dough on top of apricots to create a cobblestone effect. Bake 20 to 25 minutes or until crust is golden brown. Cool 30 minutes; then top with whipped cream and almond mixture. Makes 6 or 7 servings.

Rhubarb-Pineapple Cobbler

Instead of the proverbial rhubarb-strawberry combination, why not try rhubarb and pineapple?

Rhubarb-Pineapple Filling:

1 lb. fresh or slightly thawed frozen rhubarb, chopped in 1/2-inch pieces

1-1/2 cups fresh or drained canned pineapple chunks

3 tablespoons all-purpose flour

1-1/4 cups granulated sugar

Pinch of cinnamon

2 eggs, well-beaten

Preheat oven to 425F (220C). Grease a 9-inch-square baking dish.

Place chopped rhubarb in greased baking dish; stir in pineapple chunks. In a medium mixing bowl, whisk flour, sugar, cinnamon and eggs. Pour on top of rhubarb and pineapple; then set aside.

Brown-Sugar Shortcake Crust:

1-1/2 cups all-purpose flour
2 teaspoons baking powder
2 tablespoons granulated sugar
2 tablespoons brown sugar
1/4 cup melted butter or margarine (4 tablespoons)
1/2 cup half and half or 2% lowfat milk
Vanilla ice cream or whipped cream

In a large mixing bowl, combine crust ingredients. Stir vigorously with a wooden spoon about 30 seconds until a stiff dough forms. Spoon dough on top of rhubarb-pineapple filling to create a cobblestone effect. Bake 20 to 25 minutes or until crust is golden brown. Cool 30 minutes; then serve with vanilla ice cream or whipped cream. Makes 6 or 7 servings.

Gooseberry Cobbler

This cobbler combines a gooseberry filling with a rich, cream-cheese shortcake crust enlivened with currants and honey. Early summer is the time to look for gooseberries in the produce section although some specialty stores get their supplies from New Zealand and Chile during February.

Gooseberry Filling:

5-1/4 cups fresh gooseberries, trimmed
1-1/2 cups granulated sugar
2 tablespoons quick-cooking tapioca
2 tablespoons melted butter or margarine

Preheat oven to 425F (220C). Grease an 8-inch-square baking pan or dish.

In a large mixing bowl, carefully spoon together gooseberries, sugar and tapioca. Pour gooseberry filling into greased baking dish or pan; drizzle melted butter or margarine on top and set aside.

Cream-Cheese & Currant Shortcake Crust

1-1/2 cups all-purpose flour
2 teaspoons baking powder
1/4 cup granulated sugar
2 tablespoons honey
2 tablespoons dried currants
3/4 (3-oz.) pkg. cream cheese, softened
1/4 cup melted butter or margarine (4 tablespoons)
3/4 cup half and half or 2% lowfat milk
Whipped cream sprinkled with grated lemon rind

In another large mixing bowl, combine crust ingredients.
Stir vigorously with a wooden spoon until a stiff dough
forms. Spoon dough on top of gooseberry filling to
create a cobblestone effect. Bake 20 to 25 minutes or
until crust is golden brown. Cool 30 minutes; then serve
with whipped cream sprinkled with lemon rind. Makes
5 or 6 servings.

Crisp Cobblers

Crisp shortcake biscuit crusts made without the baking powder but with more sugar and no cream, may be crumbled on top of fruit fillings. Some pastry chefs refer to these desserts as crisps, but I like to include them in the general category of cobblers.

Raspberry-Oat Crisp Cobbler

This crunchy oat-and-nut crust complements any warm fruit filling.

Raspberry Filling:

5-1/2 cups fresh or slightly thawed frozen raspberries
1/4 cup granulated sugar
2 tablespoons quick-cooking tapioca
2 tablespoons lemon juice
2 tablespoons melted butter or margarine

Preheat oven to 375F (190C). Grease a 9-inch-square baking pan or dish.

Wash fresh raspberries thoroughly. In a large mixing bowl, carefully spoon together raspberries, sugar, tapioca and lemon juice. Pour raspberry filling into greased baking pan or dish; drizzle melted butter or margarine on top and set aside.

Walnut-Oat Crisp Crust:

1/2 cup all-purpose flour
1/2 cup quick rolled oats
1/2 cup granulated sugar
1/4 cup packed brown sugar
1/4 cup chopped walnuts
1/2 cup melted butter or margarine (1/4 lb.)
Vanilla ice cream or whipped cream

In a large bowl, combine crust ingredients. Toss lightly with a fork until dough is crumbly. Using your thumbs and fingertips, crumble dough on top of raspberry filling. Bake 35 to 40 minutes or until crust is crisp and golden brown. Cool 30 minutes; then serve with vanilla ice cream or whipped cream. Makes 6 or 7 servings.

Cherry-Date Crisp Cobbler

A little rum brings out the wonderful flavor of the cherry-date filling.

Cherry-Date Filling:

5-1/4 cups canned, pitted, red, pie cherries, drained (approximately 2-1/2 lbs.)

1/3 cup cherry juice from can

1/2 cup chopped pitted dates

1/4 cup granulated sugar

1-1/2 tablespoons quick-cooking tapioca

1 tablespoon rum or 1 teaspoon rum flavoring

2 tablespoons melted butter or margarine

Preheat oven to 375F (190C). Grease a 9-inch-square baking pan or dish.

In a large mixing bowl, carefully spoon together cherries, juice, chopped dates, sugar, tapioca and rum or flavoring. Pour cherry-date filling into greased baking pan or dish; drizzle melted butter or margarine on top and set aside.

Basic Crisp Crust:

1-1/3 cups all-purpose flour
1/2 cup granulated sugar
1/2 cup chopped pecans
1/2 cup melted butter or margarine (1/4 lb.)
Whipping cream

In another large bowl, combine crust ingredients. Toss lightly with a fork until dough is crumbly. Using your thumbs and fingertips, crumble dough on top of cherry-date filling. Bake 30 to 35 minutes or until crust is crisp and golden brown. Cool 30 minutes; then serve with a jug of cream. Makes 6 or 7 servings.

Nectarine-Maple Crisp Cobbler

Because a nectarine is a relative of the peach, it's only fitting it should be considered as a cobbler filling. Here I'm featuring it with a maple-flavored crust.

Nectarine Filling:

**10 to 12 ripe nectarines
   (about 5-1/2 cups sliced)**
1/3 cup granulated sugar
2 tablespoons quick-cooking tapioca
1 teaspoon vanilla extract
2 tablespoons melted butter or margarine

Preheat oven to 375F (190C). Grease a 9-inch-square baking pan or dish.

Before peeling, drop nectarines into very hot water about 1 minute. Peel and halve nectarines, remove pits and cut flesh into sixths. In a large mixing bowl, carefully spoon together nectarines, sugar, tapioca and vanilla. Pour nectarine filling into greased baking pan or dish; drizzle melted butter or margarine on top and set aside.

Maple Crisp Crust:

1-1/2 cups all-purpose flour
1/4 cup packed brown sugar
3 tablespoons pure maple syrup
1/4 cup chopped almonds
1/3 cup melted butter or margarine
Whipping cream

In another large bowl, combine crust ingredients. Toss lightly with a fork until dough is crumbly. Using your thumbs and fingertips, crumble dough on top of nectarine filling. Bake 35 to 40 minutes or until crust is crisp and golden brown. Cool 30 minutes; then serve with a jug of cream. Makes 6 or 7 servings.

Peach-Cinnamon Crisp

A simple and perfect peach-and-vanilla filling topped with an equally simple and perfect cinnamon crisp crust.

Peach Filling:

**10 to 12 ripe peaches or 5-1/2 cups
    sliced canned Elberta peaches, drained**
3-1/2 tablespoons granulated sugar
1-1/2 tablespoons quick-cooking tapioca
2 teaspoons vanilla extract
2 tablespoons melted butter or margarine

Preheat oven to 375F (190C). Grease a 9-inch-square baking pan or dish.

Before peeling, drop fresh peaches into very hot water about 1 minute. Peel and halve peaches, remove pits and cut flesh into sixths. In a large mixing bowl, carefully spoon together peaches, sugar, tapioca and vanilla. Pour peach filling into greased baking pan or dish; drizzle melted butter or margarine on top and set aside.

Cinnamon Crisp Crust:

1-1/3 cups all-purpose flour
1/2 cup granulated sugar
1/2 teaspoon ground cinnamon
1/2 cup chopped pecans
1/2 cup melted butter or margarine (1/4 lb.)
Whipping cream

In another large bowl, combine crust ingredients. Toss lightly with fork until dough is crumbly. Using your thumbs and fingertips, crumble dough on top of peach filling. Bake 35 to 40 minutes or until crust is crisp and golden brown. Cool 30 minutes; then serve with a jug of cream. Makes 6 or 7 servings.

Lower Fat Cobblers

If you're concerned about lowering satu-rated fats, but would never consider bypass-ing dessert, read on. I have replaced the butter and cream in these fillings and crusts with cholesterol-free canola oil and lowfat milk. Flavor accents such as chopped dried apricots, honey and spices more than make up for the reduction in richness. Lowfat vanilla yogurt makes an excellent topping instead of whipped cream or ice cream.

Blueberry Spice Cobbler

Blueberries are covered with a light, spiced biscuit.

Blueberry Filling:

5-1/4 cups fresh or slightly thawed frozen blueberries
3 tablespoons brown sugar
2 tablespoons quick-cooking tapioca
3 tablespoons lemon juice
   (juice of 1 medium-sized lemon)
1 tablespoon canola oil

Preheat oven to 425F (220C). Grease an 8-inch-square baking pan or dish.

Wash fresh blueberries thoroughly. In a large mixing bowl, carefully spoon together blueberries, brown sugar, tapioca and lemon juice. Pour blueberry filling into greased baking pan or dish; drizzle with oil and set aside.

Light & Spicy Biscuit Crust:

1-1/2 cups all-purpose flour
2 teaspoons baking powder
3 tablespoons granulated sugar
1 tablespoon honey
1/4 teaspoon ground mace
1/2 teaspoon ground cinnamon
1/4 cup canola oil
1/2 cup 2% lowfat milk
Blueberries mixed with lowfat vanilla yogurt

In another large mixing bowl, combine crust ingredients. Stir vigorously with a wooden spoon about 30 seconds until a stiff dough forms. Spoon dough on top of blueberry filling to create a cobblestone effect. Bake 20 to 25 minutes or until crust is golden brown. Cool 30 minutes; then serve with blueberry and yogurt mixture. Makes 5 or 6 servings.

Plum Cobbler

In the prime of their ripeness, dark-red plums, particularly the Santa Rosa variety, provide a succulent cobbler filling when sweetened with brown sugar and a little honey.

Plum Filling:

**5-1/4 cups thinly sliced ripe plums
  (about 2-1/2 lbs.)**
1/3 cup packed brown sugar
1 tablespoon honey
2 tablespoons quick-cooking tapioca
1 tablespoon canola oil

Preheat oven to 425F (220C). Grease a 9-inch-square baking pan or dish.

In a large mixing bowl, carefully spoon together plums, brown sugar, honey and tapioca. Pour plum filling into greased baking pan or dish; drizzle with oil and set aside.

Raisin-Oat Biscuit Crust:

1 cup all-purpose flour
1/2 cup quick rolled oats
2 teaspoons baking powder
1/2 cup granulated sugar
1-1/2 tablespoons raisins
1/4 cup canola oil
1/3 cup 2% lowfat milk

Lowfat vanilla yogurt

In another large bowl, combine flour, oats, baking powder, sugar and raisins. Gradually stir in oil and milk until dough clings together. On a lightly floured surface, gently roll out dough to fit baking pan or dish. Carefully place dough on top of plums. Cut a few slashes in dough so steam can escape. Bake 20 to 25 minutes or until golden brown. Cool 30 minutes; then serve with lowfat vanilla yogurt. Makes 6 or 7 servings.

Huckleberry-Oat-Apricot Cobbler

If you're lucky enough to find fresh huckleberries, you'll discover why many dessert chefs consider them to be the quintessential berry for pastry. Ranging in color from dark blue to black, a huckleberry is juicier than a blueberry.

Huckleberry Filling:

5-1/4 cups huckleberries or blueberries
1/2 cup honey
1 tablespoon granulated sugar
2 tablespoons quick-cooking tapioca
1 teaspoon ground cinnamon
1 tablespoon lemon juice
1 tablespoon canola oil

Preheat oven to 375F (190C). Grease an 8-inch-square baking pan or dish.

Wash huckleberries or blueberries thoroughly. In a large mixing bowl, carefully spoon together berries, honey, sugar, tapioca, cinnamon and lemon juice. Pour berry filling into greased baking pan or dish; drizzle with oil and set aside about 15 minutes.

Light Oat-Apricot Crisp Crust:

1/2 cup all-purpose flour

1/2 cup quick rolled oats

1/4 cup finely chopped dried apricots

1/4 cup finely chopped walnuts

1/2 cup granulated sugar

1/4 cup canola oil

1 teaspoon vanilla extract

Lowfat vanilla yogurt

In another large mixing bowl, combine crust ingredients. Toss lightly with a fork until dough is crumbly. Using your thumbs and fingertips, crumble dough over berry filling. Bake 35 to 40 minutes or until crust is golden brown. Cool 30 minutes; then serve with lowfat vanilla yogurt. Makes 5 or 6 servings.

Peach-Oat Cobbler

*This cobbler features an oat-and-raisin biscuit crust,
a peach filling and a topping of vanilla yogurt and
chopped dates.*

Peach Filling:

**8 to 10 ripe peaches or 5-1/4 cups
   sliced canned Elberta peaches, drained**
3-1/2 tablespoons brown sugar
2 tablespoons quick-cooking tapioca
1/2 teaspoon almond extract
1 tablespoon canola oil

Preheat oven to 425F (220C). Grease an 8-inch-square
baking pan or dish.

Before peeling, drop fresh peaches into very hot water
about 1 minute. Peel and halve peaches, remove pits and
cut flesh into sixths. In a large mixing bowl, carefully
spoon together peaches, brown sugar, tapioca and
almond extract. Pour peach filling into greased baking
pan or dish; drizzle with oil and set aside.

Light Oat-Raisin Biscuit Crust:

1 cup all-purpose flour

1/3 cup quick rolled oats

2 teaspoons baking powder

3 tablespoons granulated sugar

1/4 cup raisins

1/4 cup canola oil

1/2 cup 2% lowfat milk

Chopped dates mixed with lowfat vanilla yogurt

In another large bowl, combine crust ingredients. Stir vigorously with a wooden spoon about 30 seconds until a stiff dough forms. Spoon dough on top of peaches to create a cobblestone effect. Bake 20 to 25 minutes or until crust is golden brown. Cool 30 minutes; then serve with date-and-yogurt mixture. Makes 5 or 6 servings

Strawberry-Peach Cobbler

When baked together, fresh strawberries and peaches make a winning combination of fruit flavors.

Strawberry-Peach Filling:

**4 ripe peaches or 2 cups sliced
  canned Elberta peaches, drained**

3-1/4 cups sliced ripe strawberries

3 tablespoons brown sugar

1-1/2 tablespoons quick-cooking tapioca

1 tablespoon canola oil

Preheat oven to 425F (220C). Grease an 8-inch-square baking pan or dish.

Before peeling, drop fresh peaches into very hot water about 1 minute. Peel and halve peaches, remove pits and cut flesh into sixths. In a large mixing bowl, carefully spoon together peaches, sliced strawberries, brown sugar and tapioca. Pour fruit filling into a greased baking pan or dish; drizzle with oil and set aside.

Light Biscuit Crust:

1-1/3 cups all-purpose flour
2 teaspoons baking powder
2 tablespoons granulated sugar
1 tablespoon honey
1 teaspoon grated orange zest
1/4 cup canola oil
1/3 cup 2% lowfat milk
Lowfat vanilla yogurt

In another large bowl, combine crust ingredients. Stir vigorously with a wooden spoon about 30 seconds until a stiff dough forms. Spoon dough on top of strawberry-peach filling to create a cobblestone effect. Bake 20 to 25 minutes or until crust is golden brown. Cool 30 minutes; then serve with lowfat vanilla yogurt. Makes 5 or 6 servings.

Apple-Blueberry Cobbler

Apples and blueberries are deliciously sweet and colorful in this filling. The blueberry theme is continued in the crust.

Apple Filling:

2 to 4 apples, peeled and sliced
(3 cups or 1 lb.)
2-1/2 cups fresh or slightly thawed frozen blueberries
3 tablespoons brown sugar
2 tablespoons quick-cooking tapioca
2 teaspoons vanilla extract
1 tablespoon canola oil

Preheat oven to 425F (220C). Grease a 9-inch-square baking pan or dish.

Wash fresh blueberries thoroughly. In a large mixing bowl, carefully spoon together blueberries, apples, brown sugar, tapioca and vanilla. Pour apples and blueberries into greased baking pan or dish; drizzle oil on top and set aside.

Light Blueberry Biscuit Crust:

1-1/2 cups all-purpose flour

2 teaspoons baking powder

1/4 cup granulated sugar

1/4 teaspoon ground cinnamon

3 tablespoons fresh or slightly thawed frozen blueberries

1/4 cup canola oil or

1/2 cup 2% lowfat milk

Lowfat vanilla yogurt

In another large bowl, combine crust ingredients. Stir vigorously with a wooden spoon about 30 seconds until a stiff dough forms. Spoon dough on top of apple-blueberry filling to create a cobblestone effect. Bake 20 to 25 minutes or until crust is golden brown. Cool 30 minutes; then serve with lowfat vanilla yogurt. Makes 6 or 7 servings.

Elegant Cobblers

The most elegant cobbler desserts, particularly the creamy varieties, go best with a simple but delicious cobbler crust that tastes like rich shortbread. It is prebaked then crumbled over a rich filling.

Boysenberry-Framboise Cobbler

Framboise, a delightfully sweet raspberry liqueur, adds a special touch to any berry filling.

Boysenberry-Framboise Filling:

5-1/4 cups fresh or slightly thawed frozen boysenberries
2 tablespoons granulated sugar
2 tablespoons quick-cooking tapioca
2-1/2 tablespoons framboise or apple juice

Preheat oven to 425F (220C). Grease a 9-inch-square baking pan or dish.

In a large mixing bowl, carefully spoon together boysenberries, granulated sugar, tapioca and framboise or apple juice. Pour boysenberry filling into greased baking pan or dish; then set aside.

Brown-Sugar-Coconut Crisp Crust:

1-1/3 cups all-purpose flour
1/2 cup packed brown sugar
1/2 cup shredded coconut
1/2 cup melted butter or margarine (1/4 lb.)

Lowfat vanilla yogurt flavored with framboise

In another large bowl, combine crust ingredients. Toss lightly with a fork until dough is crumbly. Using your thumbs and fingertips, crumble dough on top of boysenberry filling. Bake 30 to 35 minutes or until crust is crisp and golden brown. Cool 30 minutes; then serve with framboise-flavored vanilla yogurt. Makes 6 or 7 servings.

Pear-Crème Cobbler

The combination of pears, sour cream and cream cheese is unforgettable when complemented with a crunchy cookie crust and a whipped cream and walnut topping. Fresh pears need to be very ripe if your cobbler is going to benefit from all the natural sweetness of the fruit.

Pear Crème Filling:

**4 cups chopped, peeled, fresh pears (about 2 lbs.)
  or 2 (29-oz.) cans pears, drained and chopped**
3 eggs
1/3 cup granulated sugar
1 (3-oz.) pkg. cream cheese, softened
1/2 cup dairy sour cream
2 tablespoons orange juice
Grated zest of 1 medium-sized orange

Preheat oven to 300F (150C). Grease a round 9-inch baking dish.

Using a blender, combine filling ingredients about 2 minutes at medium speed. Pour pear mixture into greased baking dish. Bake about 1 hour or until crème is firm. Refrigerate 1-1/2 to 2 hours.

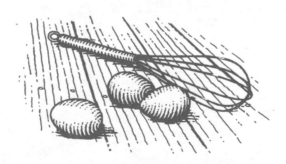

Crunchy Cookie Crust:

1-1/3 cups all-purpose flour
1/2 teaspoon baking powder
1/2 cup granulated sugar
1/2 cup melted butter or margarine (1/4 lb.)
1/4 cup whipping cream or 2% lowfat milk
1 teaspoon grated orange zest
Whipped cream and chopped walnuts

Preheat oven to 375F (190C).

In a large mixing bowl, combine crust ingredients. Using quick strokes of a fork or a handheld electric mixer set at medium speed, toss or swirl ingredients until a soft cookie dough forms. Spoon dough onto an ungreased cookie sheet. Using the back of a spoon, a knife or your fingertips, spread and flatten dough to 1/8 inch thick. Bake 15 minutes or until crust is golden brown. Set crust aside to cool at least 30 minutes before handling. Using your thumbs and fingertips, crumble cooled cookie crust over chilled pear custard. Top with whipped cream and chopped walnuts. Makes 6 or 7 servings.

Black Forest Cobbler

Made with cherries, kirsch and a crumbled chocolate crust, this Black Forest Cobbler captures the authenticity of the delicious German dessert classic.

Black Forest Cookie Crust:

1-1/3 cups all-purpose flour
1/2 teaspoon baking powder
1/3 cup unsweetened cocoa powder
1/4 cup granulated sugar
1/2 cup melted butter or margarine (1/4 lb.)
1/4 cup half and half or 2% lowfat milk

Preheat oven to 375F (190C).

In a large mixing bowl, combine crust ingredients. Using quick strokes of a fork or a handheld electric mixer set at medium speed, toss or swirl ingredients until a soft cookie dough forms. Spoon dough onto an ungreased cookie sheet. Using the back of a spoon, a knife or your fingertips, spread and flatten dough to 1/8 inch thick. Bake 15 minutes or until crust is golden brown. Set crust aside to cool at least 30 minutes before handling.

Black Forest Filling:

3 cups whipping cream (1-1/2 pints)
1/2 cup powdered sugar, sifted
2 tablespoons kirsch or 1/4 teaspoon cherry flavoring
5 cups canned, pitted, red, pie cherries, well-drained

Topping:

8 oz. semisweet chocolate
  (shaved and refrigerated until ready for use)
Whipped cream
6 to 7 maraschino cherries

In a large mixing bowl, beat cream and powdered sugar using a whisk or electric beater until cream forms peaks. Add kirsch or flavoring and beat only until liquid is absorbed. Place half of cherries in a medium-sized glass dish. Add about half of whipped-cream mixture then repeat with another layer of remaining cherries. Finish with remaining whipped-cream mixture. Using your thumbs and fingertips, crumble cooled cookie crust on top of whipped cream. Sprinkle with shaved chocolate. Decorate each serving with whipped cream and a maraschino cherry. Makes 6 or 7 servings.

Banana-Kiwi Cobbler

Bring a little sunshine to a winter meal with the tropical flavors of coconut, banana and kiwi.

Coconut Cookie Crust:

1-1/2 cups all-purpose flour
1/2 teaspoon baking powder
1/4 cup granulated sugar
1/3 cup shredded coconut
1/2 cup melted butter or margarine (1/4 lb.)
1/2 cup whipping cream or 2% lowfat milk

Preheat oven to 375F (190C).

In a large mixing bowl, combine crust ingredients. Using quick strokes of a fork or a handheld electric mixer set at medium speed, toss or swirl ingredients until a soft cookie dough forms. Spoon dough onto an ungreased cookie sheet. Using the back of a spoon, a knife or your fingertips, spread and flatten dough to 1/8 inch thick. Bake 15 minutes or until crust is golden brown. Set crust aside to cool at least 30 minutes before handling.

Banana-Kiwi Filling:

1/4 cup butter or margarine (4 tablespoons)
2 tablespoons brandy or orange juice
3 to 4 medium-sized bananas, peeled and sliced
2 tablespoons powdered sugar
4 kiwi, peeled and sliced
Whipped cream

Melt butter or margarine in a large skillet over medium heat; add brandy or orange juice. Cook bananas in brandy or juice mixture about 1 minute on each side. Lift banana slices from skillet with a slotted spoon to drain; arrange evenly in a medium-size glass dish or 9-inch pie plate. Sprinkle bananas with powdered sugar and top with sliced kiwi. Using your thumbs and fingertips, crumble cooled cookie crust over fruit. Serve with whipped cream. Makes 6 or 7 servings.

Ambrosia Cobbler

A classically delicious combination of pineapple chunks, mandarin oranges and coconut is topped with a crumbled nut crust.

Nut Cookie Crust:

1-1/3 cups all-purpose flour
1/2 teaspoon baking powder
1/2 cup granulated sugar
1/4 cup finely chopped walnuts
1/2 cup melted butter or margarine (1/4 lb.)
1/3 cup half and half or 2% lowfat milk

Preheat oven to 375F (190C).

In a large mixing bowl, combine crust ingredients. Using quick strokes of a fork or a handheld electric mixer set at medium speed, toss or swirl ingredients until a soft cookie dough forms. Spoon dough onto an ungreased cookie sheet. Using the back of a spoon, a knife or your fingertips, spread and flatten dough to 1/8 inch thick. Bake 15 minutes or until crust is golden brown. Set crust aside to cool at least 30 minutes before handling.

Orange-Pineapple Filling:

1-1/2 cups drained mandarin oranges
1-1/4 cups fresh or drained canned pineapple chunks
1/4 cup honey
1/2 cup shredded coconut
Vanilla ice cream, vanilla yogurt or whipped cream

In a medium-size glass dish or a 9-inch pie plate, mix mandarin oranges and pineapple chunks. Drizzle honey on top of fruit; then sprinkle with coconut. Using your thumbs and fingertips, crumble cooled cookie crust on top of fruit. Serve with vanilla ice cream, vanilla yogurt or whipped cream. Makes 6 or 7 servings.

Holiday Cobblers

For a new twist on holiday favorites, treat your guests to crumb-topped Pumpkin-Mousse Cobbler or the Cranberry Crunch Cobbler made with a rich and crunchy corn-meal crust.

Pumpkin-Mousse Cobbler

There is a hint of ginger in the crumbs which cover this creamy mousse.

Pumpkin Filling:
2 teaspoons gelatin
2 tablespoons cold water
1/4 cup boiling water
1 (16-oz.) can pumpkin puree
1 cup powdered sugar, sifted
1/4 teaspoon ground cinnamon
2 cups whipping cream (1 pint)

In a small bowl, soak gelatin in cold water until softened. Stir in boiling water until gelatin has dissolved; set aside. In a large mixing bowl, beat pumpkin puree, powdered sugar and cinnamon until blended. Whisk gelatin into pumpkin mixture. In a large bowl, whip cream until stiff; fold into pumpkin mixture. Pour into a medium-sized glass dish. Refrigerate 1-1/2 hours.

Crunchy Cookie Crust:

1-1/3 cups all-purpose flour
1/2 teaspoon baking powder
1/4 teaspoon ground ginger
1/2 cup packed brown sugar
1/2 cup melted butter or margarine (1/4 lb.)
1/4 cup whipping cream or 2% lowfat milk
Whipped cream flavored with grated nutmeg

Preheat oven to 375F (190C).

In a large mixing bowl, combine crust ingredients. Using quick strokes of a fork or a handheld electric mixer set at medium speed, toss or swirl ingredients until a soft cookie dough forms. Spoon dough onto an ungreased cookie sheet. Using the back of a spoon, a knife or your fingertips, spread and flatten dough to 1/8 inch thick. Bake 15 minutes or until crust is golden brown. Set crust aside to cool at least 30 minutes before handling. Using your thumbs and fingertips, crumble cooled cookie crust over chilled pumpkin mousse. Serve with whipped cream flavored with nutmeg. Makes 6 or 7 servings.

Sweet-Potato Cobbler

One taste of this spicy cobbler may make you forget pumpkin pie ever existed. The praline cookie crust is a fitting Southern touch.

Sweet-Potato Filling:

3 large sweet potatoes, cooked (about 2-1/4 cups pulp)
1/4 cup granulated sugar
1/4 cup powdered sugar
1-1/2 tablespoons brown sugar
1/4 teaspoon grated nutmeg
1/4 teaspoon ground cinnamon
1/4 teaspoon ground cloves
1/8 teaspoon salt
2 eggs, well-beaten
1-2/3 cups whipping cream or evaporated milk

Preheat oven to 425F (220C). Grease a 9-inch-square baking dish.

In a large bowl, combine sweet-potato pulp, granulated sugar, powdered sugar, brown sugar, nutmeg, cinnamon, cloves and salt. Using a handheld electric mixer set at medium speed, beat in eggs and cream or evaporated milk until smooth. Pour into greased baking dish. Bake 15 minutes. Reduce oven temperature to 350F (175C). Bake 40 minutes longer or until a fork inserted in center comes out clean. Cool at least 2 hours at room temperature or in the refrigerator.

Praline Cookie Crust:

1-1/3 cups all-purpose flour
1/2 teaspoon baking powder
1/4 cup granulated sugar
1/4 cup packed brown sugar
1/2 cup finely chopped pecans
1/2 cup melted butter or margarine (1/4 lb.)
1/4 cup whipping cream or 2% lowfat milk
1-1/2 teaspoons rum or 1/2 teaspoon rum flavoring
Whipped cream

Preheat oven to 375F (190C).

In a large mixing bowl, combine crust ingredients. Using quick strokes of a fork or a handheld electric mixer set at medium speed, toss or swirl ingredients until a soft cookie dough forms. Spoon dough onto an ungreased cookie sheet. Using the back of a spoon, a knife or your fingertips, spread and flatten dough to 1/8 inch thick. Bake 15 minutes or until crust is golden brown. Set crust aside to cool at least 30 minutes before handling. Using your thumbs and fingertips, crumble cooled cookie crust over cooled sweet-potato filling. Serve with whipped cream. Makes 6 or 7 servings.

Cranberry Crunch Cobbler

Cornmeal in the crust adds extra crunch and color to this holiday cobbler which is served with a tangy lemon sauce.

Cranberry Filling:

5-1/4 cups fresh cranberries
1-1/4 cups granulated sugar
2 tablespoons quick-cooking tapioca
1 tablespoon grated lemon zest
1-1/2 tablespoons melted butter or margarine

Grease a 9-inch-square baking dish.

Bring 2 quarts water to boil in a large pot. Place cranberries in boiling water until soft, about 3 minutes; drain. In a large mixing bowl, carefully spoon together cranberries, sugar, tapioca and lemon zest. Pour cranberry filling into greased baking dish; drizzle with melted butter or margarine and set aside.

Cornbread Crust:

1 cup all-purpose flour
1/2 cup yellow or white stone-ground cornmeal
2 teaspoons baking powder
1/4 cup granulated sugar
1/4 cup melted butter or margarine (4 tablespoons)
1 egg, well-beaten
1/4 cup whipping cream or 2% lowfat milk

Preheat oven to 400F (205C).

In another large mixing bowl, combine crust ingredients. Stir vigorously with a wooden spoon about 30 seconds until a soft dough forms. Drop spoonfuls of cornmeal dough on top of cranberries to create a cobblestone effect. Bake 25 to 30 minutes or until crust is golden brown. Cool 30 minutes before serving with sauce.

Lemon Sauce:

1/2 cup powdered sugar
2 teaspoons grated lemon zest
1 tablespoon quick-cooking tapioca
1/4 cup melted butter or margarine (4 tablespoons)
1 cup lemon juice

In a medium saucepan over medium heat, whisk sauce ingredients until blended. Cook until sauce begins to bubble. Cool to room temperature. Serve sauce with cooled cobbler. Makes 6 or 7 servings.

Mincemeat & Cream-Cheese Cobbler

Apples and green tomatoes flavor this festive filling. Cream cheese, brown sugar and cinnamon enhance the shortcake biscuit crust.

Mincemeat Filling:

3 tablespoons butter or margarine

3 medium-size green apples, peeled and sliced (3 cups or 1 lb.)

1-1/2 cups sliced, seeded green tomatoes

1 cup raisins

1/2 cup granulated sugar

1/4 teaspoon ground cloves

1/4 teaspoon ground allspice

2 tablespoons lemon juice

1/2 teaspoon cornstarch

1 tablespoon brandy

Grease a round 9-inch baking dish.

Melt butter or margarine in a large saucepan over low heat. Add sliced apples, tomatoes and raisins; simmer until soft. Stir in granulated sugar, cloves, allspice and lemon juice. Sprinkle cornstarch over apple mixture. Add brandy and continue stirring until cornstarch is well blended. Pour mincemeat filling into greased baking dish and set aside.

Cinnamon-Cream-Cheese Shortcake Crust:

1-1/2 cups all-purpose flour
2 teaspoons baking powder
1/4 cup packed brown sugar
1 teaspoon ground cinnamon
3/4 (3-oz.) pkg. cream cheese, softened
1/4 cup melted butter or margarine (4 tablespoons)
3/4 cup whole milk or 2% lowfat milk

Whipped cream

Preheat oven to 425F (220C).

In a large bowl, combine crust ingredients. Stir vigorously with a wooden spoon about 30 seconds until a stiff dough forms. Spoon cream-cheese dough on top of mincemeat filling to create a cobblestone effect. Bake 20 to 25 minutes or until golden brown. Cool 30 minutes; then serve with whipped cream. Makes 6 or 7 servings.

Sicilian Cassata Cobbler

This is my version of the popular Sicilian dessert. Traditionally, cassata is served during Christmas and Easter with steaming cups of coffee which have been flavored with anisette, a licorice liqueur.

Lemon Cookie Crust:

1-1/3 cups all-purpose flour
1/4 teaspoon baking soda
1/4 teaspoon baking powder
1/2 cup granulated sugar
1/2 cup melted butter or margarine (1/4 lb.)
1-1/2 tablespoons grated lemon zest
1/4 cup half and half or 2% lowfat milk

Preheat oven to 375F (190C).

In a large bowl, combine crust ingredients. Using quick strokes of a fork or a handheld electric mixer set at medium speed, toss or swirl ingredients until a soft cookie dough forms. Spoon dough onto an ungreased cookie sheet. Using the back of a spoon, a knife or your fingertips, spread and flatten dough to 1/8 inch thick. Bake 15 minutes or until crust is golden brown. Set crust aside to cool at least 30 minutes before handling.

Cassata Filling:

1 lb. ricotta cheese
2 tablespoons whipping cream or 2% lowfat milk
1/4 cup granulated sugar
3 tablespoons Grand Marnier or orange juice
1/3 cup semisweet chocolate chips
1/4 cup finely chopped candied fruit
3 tablespoons shredded coconut

Using a fork or a handheld electric mixer, blend ricotta cheese, cream or milk, sugar and Grand Marnier or juice until smooth. Fold in chocolate chips, candied fruit and coconut. Spoon ricotta filling into a medium-sized glass dish. Using your thumbs and fingertips, crumble cooled cookie crust on top of cassata filling.

Chocolate-Espresso Topping:

12 oz. semisweet chocolate, cut into small pieces
3/4 cup hot espresso
1/2 lb. butter or margarine, chilled and cut into
** small pieces**

In a small saucepan, melt chocolate in hot espresso over low heat, stirring constantly. Remove from heat. Whisk in butter or margarine until completely smooth. Refrigerate until thickened. Using a spatula, spread cooled topping over crumbled cookie crust. Makes 6 or 7 servings.

Custard & Cream Cobblers

Crunchy cookie crusts made with a touch of baking powder provide the perfect texture contrast to cool and creamy fillings. Try these cobblers as summer desserts.

Banana-Cream Cobbler

This cobbler is pure banana heaven.

Cream Filling:
2/3 cup granulated sugar
1/2 cup all-purpose flour
Pinch of salt
2 cups half and half (1 pint)
3 egg yolks
2 tablespoons melted butter or margarine
1 teaspoon vanilla extract
3 large or 4 small bananas
1/4 cup orange juice

In a large mixing bowl, beat sugar, flour, salt, half and half, egg yolks, butter or margarine and vanilla until blended. In a medium saucepan over medium heat, whisk cream mixture frequently until it gently boils and thickens. Remove from heat and cool about 20 minutes.

Slice bananas into an ungreased 9-inch-square dish. Spoon over orange juice and gently mix until bananas are coated with juice. Pour cooled cream over bananas. Refrigerate at least 2 hours.

Crunchy Cookie Crust:

1-1/3 cups all-purpose flour
1/2 teaspoon baking powder
1/2 cup granulated sugar
1/2 cup melted butter or margarine (1/4 lb.)
1/4 cup half and half or 2% lowfat milk
Grated zest of 1 orange

Whipped cream

Preheat oven to 375F (190C).

In a large mixing bowl, combine crust ingredients. Using quick strokes of a fork or a handheld electric mixer set at medium speed, toss or swirl ingredients until a soft cookie dough forms. Spoon dough onto an ungreased cookie sheet. Using the back of a spoon, a knife or your fingertips, spread and flatten dough to 1/8 inch thick. Bake 15 minutes or until crust is golden brown. Set crust aside to cool at least 30 minutes before handling. Using your thumbs and fingertips, crumble cooled cookie crust over chilled cream filling. Serve cobbler with whipped cream. Makes 6 or 7 servings.

Lemonade-Raspberry Cobbler

Lemonade and fresh raspberries are well-matched combatants for strong tart and sweet flavors. A great favorite with children especially when served in individual pudding cups.

Lemonade Filling:

1-1/2 cups whipping cream
1 (14-oz.) can sweetened condensed milk
1 (10-1/2-oz.) can thawed frozen lemonade

In a large mixing bowl, beat cream with an electric beater at medium-high speed until thick and peaks start forming. Then reduce speed and gently mix in condensed milk and lemonade until well blended. Pour lemonade cream into a 9-inch-square dish. Refrigerate 1½ hours.

Brown-Sugar Crunchy Cookie Crust:

1-1/3 cups all-purpose flour
1/4 teaspoon baking soda
1/4 teaspoon baking powder
1/3 cup packed brown sugar
1/2 cup melted butter or margarine (1/4 lb.)
1/4 cup buttermilk

Topping:

1 cup fresh raspberries

Preheat oven to 375F (190C).

In another large bowl, combine crust ingredients.Using quick strokes of a fork or a handheld electric mixer set at medium speed, toss or swirl ingredients until a soft cookie dough forms. Spoon dough onto an ungreased cookie sheet. Using the back of a spoon, a knife or your fingertips, spread and flatten dough to 1/8 inch thick. Bake 15 minutes or until crust is golden brown. Set crust aside to cool at least 30 minutes before handling. Cover chilled lemonade filling with a thin layer of raspberries. Using your thumbs and fingertips, crumble cooled cookie crust over raspberries. Serve immediately. Makes 6 or 7 servings.

Crème-Brûlée Cobbler

Here's a rich custard cobbler glazed with a caramel-walnut sauce and topped with a crunchy cookie crust.

Crème-Brûlée Filling:

1-1/2 pints whipping cream (3 cups)
1/4 cup granulated sugar
6 egg yolks, well-beaten
1 tablespoon maple syrup

Preheat oven to 325F (165C). Lightly grease an 8-inch-square baking dish.

In a double boiler, heat cream over boiling water. Reduce heat so water simmers. Whisk sugar, beaten egg yolks and maple syrup into cream. Continue stirring until mixture begins to thicken. Pour cream filling into lightly greased baking dish. Set dish in a large baking pan holding 1/2 inch of water. Bake 20 minutes or until firm. Refrigerate 6 hours.

Crunchy Cookie Crust:

1-1/3 cups all-purpose flour
1/2 teaspoon baking powder
1/2 cup granulated sugar
1/2 cup melted butter or margarine (1/4 lb.)
1/4 cup whipping cream or 2% lowfat milk

Preheat oven to 375F (190C).

In a large mixing bowl, combine crust ingredients. Using quick strokes of a fork or a handheld mixer set at medium speed, toss or swirl ingredients until a soft cookie dough forms. Spoon dough onto an ungreased cookie sheet. Using the back of a spoon, a knife or your fingertips, spread and flatten dough to 1/8 inch thick. Bake 15 minutes or until crust is golden brown. Set crust aside to cool at least 30 minutes before handling.

Caramel-Walnut Topping:

1 cup whipping cream
1-1/2 cups packed brown sugar
1/2 cup corn syrup
1/2 cup chopped walnuts

About 1 hour before serving, begin preparing topping. In a large saucepan, bring cream to a boil. Remove from heat and gradually stir in brown sugar and corn syrup. Return to low heat stirring constantly about 2 minutes. Stir in chopped walnuts. Cool to room temperature then pour over chilled filling. Using your thumbs and fingertips, crumble cooled cookie crust over topping. Makes 6 or 7 servings.

Fresh-Coconut-Cream Cobbler

Fresh coconut gives an interesting texture and extra flavor to this exotic cobbler.

Coconut-Cream Filling:

1 medium-size fresh coconut
2/3 cup granulated sugar
3 tablespoons all-purpose flour
Pinch of salt
2 cups half and half (1 pint)
3 egg yolks
2 tablespoons melted butter or margarine
1 teaspoon vanilla extract

Preheat oven to 350F (175C).

Using an ice pick, pierce the 3 black dots on the peak of the coconut. Drain all liquid. Place coconut in preheated oven 15 minutes. Set aside to cool, then wrap in a cloth. Using a hammer, crack enclosed coconut into pieces and separate shell and skin from meat. Towel dry coconut meat. Using a hand grater or food processor, shred all white meat and set aside. In a large bowl, whisk sugar, flour, salt, half and half, egg yolks, butter or margarine and vanilla until blended. Pour into a medium saucepan over low heat. Whisk yolk mixture frequently until it gently boils and thickens. Remove from heat; then stir in grated coconut. Pour coconut cream into a 9-inch-square dish. Refrigerate at least 2 hours.

Crunchy Cookie Crust:

1-1/3 cups all-purpose flour
1/2 teaspoon baking powder
1/2 cup granulated sugar
1/2 cup melted butter or margarine (1/4 lb.)
1/4 cup half and half or 2% lowfat milk
Whipped cream

Preheat oven to 375F (190C).

In a large mixing bowl, combine crust ingredients. Using quick strokes of a fork or with a handheld electric mixer set at medium speed, toss or swirl ingredients until a soft cookie dough forms. Spoon dough onto an ungreased cookie sheet. Using the back of a spoon, a knife or your fingertips, spread and flatten dough to 1/8 inch thick. Bake 15 minutes or until crust is golden brown. Set crust aside to cool at least 30 minutes before handling. Just before serving, crumble cooled crust over chilled coconut filling using your thumb and fingertips. Top with whipped cream. Makes 6 or 7 servings.

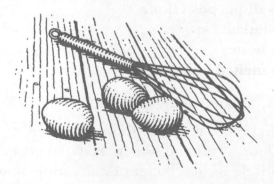

Cake Cobblers

Egg added to the cobbler crust makes it slightly cakey, moist and lighter in texture than the shortcake and biscuit crusts.

Strawberry-Rhubarb Cake Cobbler

The pairing of strawberries with rhubarb is typically associated with a pie, but here I am using this classic sweet-and-tart combination as a filling for a cake cobbler crust with shredded coconut.

Strawberry-Rhubarb Filling:

2 cups fresh or slightly thawed frozen rhubarb, chopped in 1/2-inch pieces
2-1/2 cups sliced strawberries
3 tablespoons all-purpose flour
1-1/4 cups granulated sugar
3 tablespoons honey
2 tablespoons melted butter or margarine

Grease a 9-inch-square baking dish.

In a large mixing bowl, combine rhubarb, sliced strawberries, flour, sugar and honey. Place in greased baking dish; drizzle melted butter or margarine on top and set aside.

Basic Cake Crust:

1-1/3 cups all-purpose flour
2-1/2 teaspoons baking powder
2 tablespoons granulated sugar
2 tablespoons brown sugar
1/2 cup shredded coconut, if desired
1/4 cup melted butter or margarine
2 eggs, well-beaten
1/4 cup whipping cream or 2% lowfat milk
Whipped cream sprinkled with grated orange zest

Preheat oven to 400F (205C).

In another large bowl, combine crust ingredients. Stir vigorously with a wooden spoon until a soft dough forms. Drop spoonfuls of batter on top of strawberry-rhubarb filling; spread evenly with a spatula to cover. Bake 25 minutes or until a toothpick inserted in center comes out clean. Cool 30 minutes; then serve with whipped cream sprinkled with orange zest. Makes 6 or 7 servings.

Peach-Pistachio Cake Cobbler

A sprinkling of pistachios and ginger adds color and excitement to this cake crust.

Peach-Pistachio Filling:

10 to 12 ripe peaches or 5-1/2 cups sliced canned Elberta peaches, drained

1/4 cup packed brown sugar

2 tablespoons chopped pistachios

2 tablespoons quick-cooking tapioca

2 teaspoons vanilla extract

2 tablespoons melted butter or margarine

Preheat oven to 400F (205C). Grease a 9-inch-square baking pan or dish.

Before peeling, drop fresh peaches into very hot water about 1 minute. Peel and halve peaches, remove pits and cut flesh into sixths. In a large mixing bowl, carefully spoon together peaches, brown sugar, pistachios, tapioca and vanilla. Pour peach filling into greased baking pan or dish; drizzle melted butter or margarine on top and set aside.

Ginger Cake Crust:

1-1/3 cups all-purpose flour
2-1/2 teaspoons baking powder
1/4 cup granulated sugar
2 tablespoons chopped pistachios
1/4 teaspoon ground ginger
1/3 cup melted butter or margarine
2 eggs, well-beaten
1/4 cup whipping cream or 2% lowfat milk

Vanilla ice cream or whipped cream

In another large bowl, combine crust ingredients. Stir vigorously with a wooden spoon until a soft dough forms. Drop spoonfuls of batter on top of peaches; spread evenly with a spatula to cover. Bake 25 minutes or until a toothpick inserted in center comes out clean. Cool 30 minutes; then serve with vanilla ice cream or whipped cream. Makes 6 or 7 servings.

Cherry-Apple-Cinnamon Cake Cobbler

Here's a cobbler featuring cherries, apples and a cinnamon cake crust. Using canned cherries, this dessert can be served any time of year.

Cherry Filling:

4 cups canned, pitted, red, pie cherries, drained (about 2 lbs.)

1/2 cup cherry juice from can

1 to 2 tart apples, peeled and sliced (1 cup)

1/4 cup granulated sugar

1-1/2 tablespoons quick-cooking tapioca

2 tablespoons melted butter or margarine

Preheat oven to 400F (205C). Grease a 9-inch-square baking pan or dish.

In a large mixing bowl, carefully spoon together cherries, juice, sliced apple, sugar and tapioca. Pour cherry filling into greased baking pan or dish; drizzle melted butter or margarine on top and set aside.

Cinnamon Cake Crust:

1-1/3 cups all-purpose flour
2-1/2 teaspoons baking powder
1/4 cup granulated sugar
1/3 cup melted butter or margarine
2 eggs, well-beaten
1/4 cup whipping cream or 2% lowfat milk
1 tablespoon melted butter or margarine
2 tablespoons granulated sugar
1 teaspoon ground cinnamon
Whipped cream

In another large bowl, combine flour, baking powder, 1/4 cup sugar, 1/3 cup melted butter or margarine, eggs and cream or milk. Stir vigorously with a wooden spoon until a soft dough forms. Drop spoonfuls of batter on top of cherries; spread evenly with a spatula to cover. Drizzle 1 tablespoon melted butter or margarine on top of batter; then sprinkle on 2 tablespoons sugar and cinnamon. Bake 25 minutes or until a toothpick inserted in center comes out clean. Cool 30 minutes; then serve with whipped cream. Makes 6 or 7 servings.

Raspberry-Chocolate Cake Cobbler

This special-occasion cobbler combines raspberries, a rich cake crust and the crowning touch—a sinful chocolate topping.

Raspberry Filling:

2 (12-oz.) pkgs. slightly thawed frozen raspberries
1/3 cup packed brown sugar
1 teaspoon ground cinnamon
2 tablespoons quick-cooking tapioca
2 tablespoons melted butter or margarine

Preheat oven to 400F (205C). Grease a 9-inch-square baking dish.

In a large mixing bowl, carefully spoon together raspberries, brown sugar, cinnamon and tapioca. Pour raspberry filling into greased baking dish; drizzle melted butter or margarine on top and set aside.

Sour-Cream Cake Crust:

1-1/3 cups all-purpose flour
2-1/2 teaspoons baking powder
1/4 cup granulated sugar
1/3 cup melted butter or margarine
2 eggs, well-beaten
1/4 cup dairy sour cream

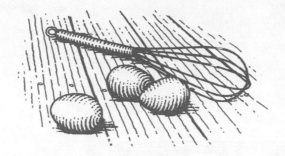

In another large bowl, combine crust ingredients. Stir vigorously with a wooden spoon until a soft dough forms. Drop spoonfuls of batter on top of raspberries; spread evenly with a spatula to cover. Bake 25 minutes or until a toothpick inserted in center comes out clean. Cool 30 minutes, then spread chocolate topping over crust just before serving.

Chocolate Topping:
4 oz. semisweet chocolate
2 tablespoons butter or margarine
1/2 cup powdered sugar, sifted
2 tablespoons whole milk or 2% lowfat milk

In a small saucepan, melt chocolate and butter or margarine over low heat. Remove from heat and add powdered sugar and milk; stir until smooth. Set aside to cool completely. Spread cooled topping over cooled cobbler crust. Makes 6 or 7 servings.

Savory Cobblers

Savory, non-sweet cobblers make ideal do-ahead entrees for brunch, lunch or dinner. Many fillings can be prepared ahead and refrigerated while dry crust ingredients can be measured and set aside. Close to serving time add liquid ingredients to the crust and assemble your cobbler.

Despite the common perception of the cobbler as a dessert, cobblers originated as savory breakfast dishes. Over open-flame hearths, American colonists gently simmered their hearty cobblers in Dutch ovens for the first meal of the day. Although early documented versions contained warm fruit, many types of fillings may be considered for complementing a late and leisurely breakfast, a light lunch or a hearty supper.

Brunch Cobblers

Try serving one or more of these tasty savory cobblers as featured hot dishes at your next brunch. Platters of sliced fruit and cheeses, a selection of raw vegetables, and fresh flowers will complete your party table.

Welsh-Rarebit Cobbler with Fresh Asparagus

Traditionally served over toast, I have combined this tasty cheese classic with a crunchy crust.

Welsh-Rarebit Filling:

1-1/2 lbs. fresh asparagus
3 tablespoons butter or margarine
3 tablespoons all-purpose flour
1-1/4 cups beer or ale
2 eggs, well-beaten
2 cups shredded Cheddar cheese (1/2 lb.)
1 teaspoon Worcestershire sauce
1 teaspoon dry mustard
1/2 teaspoon celery salt
Pinch of curry powder
Salt and pepper to taste
1/2 cup chopped tomatoes

Lightly grease a 9-inch-square baking dish.

Wash asparagus. Snap off and discard lower stalks.
Cook asparagus in a steamer or a shallow pan of boiling
water until tender. Drain then chop into 2-inch lengths;
set aside. In a medium saucepan, whisk butter or
margarine and flour over medium heat. Reduce heat to
low and stir in remaining ingredients for filling except
tomatoes. Whisk frequently until sauce is smooth and
thickened, 5 to 7 minutes. Gently stir in cooked
asparagus and tomatoes. Pour into lightly greased
baking dish and set aside.

Whole-Wheat Crust:

1 cup all-purpose flour
1/3 cup stone-ground whole-wheat flour
1 tablespoon wheat germ
1-1/2 teaspoons baking powder
1/2 teaspoon baking soda
1/2 teaspoon salt
1/4 cup melted butter or margarine (4 tablespoons)
1/3 cup buttermilk

Preheat oven to 425F (220C).

In a large mixing bowl, combine crust ingredients. Toss
lightly with a fork until dough clings together. On a
lightly floured surface, roll out dough to 1/2 inch thick.
Using a 1-1/2-inch cutter dipped in flour, cut out about
12 biscuits. Arrange over cheese filling. Bake 20 to 25
minutes or until biscuits are golden brown. Cool 5
minutes before serving. Makes 6 or 7 servings.

Zwiebelkuchen Cobbler

In Freiburg, Germany at each October harvest celebration, local wine is served with slices of a favorite Black Forest onion pie. My lighter version makes a wonderful brunch or supper dish.

Rye-Caraway Crust:

2 cups finely milled rye flour
1 teaspoon baking powder
1 teaspoon salt
1-1/2 tablespoons caraway seeds
3/4 cup melted butter or margarine
1/2 cup half and half or 2% lowfat milk

Preheat oven to 425F (220C). Lightly grease a 13" x 9" baking pan or dish.

In a large bowl, combine crust ingredients. Stir vigorously with a wooden spoon about 30 seconds until a stiff dough forms. Using your fingers, stretch and shape dough to completely cover bottom of lightly greased baking pan or dish. Bake cobbler shell 10 minutes; then set aside to cool.

Onion & Ham Custard Filling:

**1/2 lb. Black Forest ham* or Canadian bacon,
  thinly sliced**
2 tablespoons canola oil or safflower oil
4 medium-size yellow onions, finely chopped
**2 cups diced Emmentaler, Gruyère or Swiss cheese
  (1/2 lb.)**
3 eggs, well-beaten

*Available at many specialty delicatessens.

1 cup dairy sour cream
1/2 cup plain lowfat yogurt
1/2 teaspoon cornstarch
2 teaspoons finely chopped chives
Sliced tomatoes, if desired
Halved pitted black olives, if desired

Cut ham or bacon in 1-inch strips. Heat oil in a medium skillet over medium heat; add ham or bacon and chopped onions. Sauté until onions are soft; drain thoroughly. Sprinkle cooked ham or bacon, onions and diced cheese over baked crust. In a large mixing bowl, whisk beaten eggs, sour cream, yogurt, cornstarch and chopped chives about 1 minute until blended. Pour over onion mixture in crust. Reduce oven heat to 375F (190C) and bake 25 minutes or until center of custard is firm to the touch. Top baked custard with sliced tomatoes and halved black olives before serving, if desired. Serve warm. Makes 8 or 9 servings.

Artichoke Cobbler

Tender artichoke hearts, ham, Jarlsburg cheese and crunchy walnuts are combined under a crumb topping for a lovely brunch dish.

Artichoke Filling:

2 tablespoons olive oil

2 (9-oz.) pkgs. thawed frozen artichoke hearts, well-drained

2 oz. chopped cooked ham

1/4 cup finely chopped shallots or green onions

Salt and pepper to taste

1/4 cup chopped pimiento

1/4 teaspoon dried dill

1 tablespoon chopped fresh parsley

1/4 cup chopped walnuts

1/2 cup shredded Jarlsburg cheese (2 oz.)

2 eggs, well-beaten

1-1/2 cups half and half or 2% lowfat milk

Preheat oven to 375F (190C). Grease a 9-inch-square baking dish.

In a large skillet, heat oil over low heat. Add artichoke hearts, ham, shallots or green onions, salt and pepper; cook, stirring frequently, about 2 minutes. Spoon artichoke mixture into greased baking dish; sprinkle with pimiento, dill, parsley and walnuts. In a medium-sized bowl, combine Jarlsburg cheese, eggs and half and half or milk. Pour over artichoke mixture; then set aside.

Parmesan Crumb Topping:

3/4 cup all-purpose flour
1/2 teaspoon garlic powder
1/4 cup grated Parmesan cheese (1 oz.)
3 tablespoons melted butter or margarine

In a large mixing bowl, combine topping ingredients. Toss with a fork until crumbly. Using your thumbs and fingertips, crumble dough on top of artichoke filling. Bake 25 to 30 minutes or until crust is golden brown. Serve immediately. Makes 5 or 6 servings.

Turkey-Tetrazzini Cobbler

Although this dish is named after opera singer Luisa Tetrazzini, its origin is definitely American. Instead of the vermicelli, I am featuring an herb biscuit crust.

Turkey-Tetrazzini Filling:

1/4 cup butter or margarine
1-1/2 tablespoons all-purpose flour
2 cups chopped fresh mushrooms (1/2 lb. or 6 large)
4 thinly sliced celery stalks
1 cup turkey or chicken broth
1 cup half and half or 2% lowfat milk
2 egg yolks, well-beaten
2 tablespoons sherry
3-1/2 cups cubed, cooked, skinned turkey
Salt and pepper to taste
1/4 cup grated Parmesan cheese (1 oz.)

Grease a 13" x 9" baking pan or dish.

In a large saucepan, melt butter or margarine over low heat. Whisk in flour; increase heat to medium and add mushrooms, celery, broth, cream, egg yolks and sherry. Increase heat and bring to a boil, stir in turkey, salt and pepper. Pour into greased baking pan or dish; sprinkle Parmesan cheese on top and set aside.

Cornbread Herb Crust:

1 cup all-purpose flour
1 cup yellow or white stone-ground cornmeal
2-1/2 teaspoons baking powder
2 tablespoons granulated sugar
1 teaspoon Italian seasoning
Pinch of salt
1/4 cup melted butter or margarine (4 tablespoons)
1/2 cup whole milk or 2% lowfat milk
1 egg, well-beaten

Preheat oven to 400F (205C).

In a large bowl, combine crust ingredients. Stir vigorously with a wooden spoon about 30 seconds until a soft dough forms. Spoon herb dough over turkey filling to create a cobblestone effect. Bake 30 to 35 minutes or until a toothpick inserted in center comes out clean. Cool 5 minutes before serving. Makes 8 to 10 servings.

Southern Italian Sausage & Onion Cobbler

This filling is an adaptation of a recipe from Basilicata, a Southern Italian region. It features sweet Italian sausages, tomatoes and peppers.

Marinara Sauce:

1/4 cup olive oil
1/4 cup finely chopped green onions
1 carrot, grated
1 garlic clove, minced
1 (28-oz.) can crushed tomatoes
2 tablespoons tomato puree
3/4 cup water
3/4 cup dry red wine
1 tablespoon finely chopped fresh basil or
   2 teaspoons dried-leaf basil
1/2 teaspoon dried-leaf oregano
1 teaspoon granulated sugar

In a large saucepan, heat oil over medium heat. Add green onions, carrot and garlic and sauté about 2 minutes. Stir in tomatoes, tomato puree, water, wine, basil, oregano and sugar. Reduce heat to low; simmer sauce uncovered about 30 minutes, stirring occasionally.

Sausage & Pepper Filling:

1-1/4 lbs. Italian sausage links, cut apart
1 medium-size yellow onion, diced
1 green bell pepper, seeded and sliced
1 red bell pepper, seeded and sliced

While sauce simmers, start preparing sausage filling. Cut sausage links into 1-1/2-inch pieces. In a large skillet over medium heat, cook sausages 2 to 3 minutes until browned. Add onion and peppers, stirring constantly until softened. Drain thoroughly. Place sausage mixture in a 9-inch-square baking pan or dish. Pour in Marinara Sauce.

Romano-Cheese Biscuit Crust:

1-1/2 cups all-purpose flour
2 teaspoons baking powder
2 tablespoons finely chopped chives
1 tablespoon finely chopped fresh basil or
  1 teaspoon dried-leaf basil
Pinch of dried-leaf thyme
1-1/2 tablespoons grated Romano cheese
1/2 cup melted butter or margarine (1/4 lb.)
1/3 cup whipping cream or 2% lowfat milk

Preheat oven to 425F (220C).

In a large mixing bowl, combine crust ingredients. Stir vigorously with a wooden spoon about 30 seconds until a stiff dough forms. Spoon dough on top of sausage filling to create a cobblestone effect. Bake 20 to 25 minutes or until crust is golden brown. Cool 5 minutes before serving. Makes 8 or 9 servings.

Sausage & Apple Cobbler

This hearty dish combines the spicy flavor of country sausage with the pungent tart and sweet flavors of apples and onions. The crust is slightly sweet. If you like sausages and bacon served on the side of pancakes or waffles, you'll love this brunch cobbler.

1-1/2 lbs. bulk pork sausage
1 large onion, sliced
2 cups sliced apple (about 3 medium apples)
1/4 cup golden raisins
2 teaspoons cornstarch
6 tablespoons brown sugar
1 cup apple juice or water

In a large skillet, cook sausage over medium heat until completely brown. Drain skillet of all liquid; then reduce heat to low and add sliced onion and apples. Cook, stirring frequently 10 to 12 minutes or until onion is softened. Stir in raisins. In a small bowl, whisk cornstarch, brown sugar and juice or water until smooth. Stir into sausage mixture. Spoon sausage filling into an ungreased 10-inch-square baking dish or pan; set aside to cool.

Sage Biscuit Crust:

1-1/2 cups all-purpose flour
2 teaspoons baking powder
2-1/2 tablespoons granulated sugar
1/2 teaspoon rubbed sage
1/4 cup melted butter or margarine (4 tablespoons)
1/3 cup half and half or 2% lowfat milk

Preheat oven to 425F (220C).

In a large mixing bowl, combine crust ingredients. Stir vigorously with a wooden spoon about 30 seconds until a stiff dough forms. Spoon dough around edge of sausage filling. Bake 20 to 25 minutes or until crust is golden brown. Cool 5 minutes before serving. Makes 8 servings.

Pain-Perdu Berry Cobbler

Pain perdu is a Creole creation known to many as French toast. My version is made with fresh or leftover buttermilk biscuits fried to a delicious golden brown and sprinkled with powdered sugar, cinnamon, nutmeg and a squeeze of lemon.

Dough for Green-Onion Buttermilk Biscuits, page 141, made without green onions and salt, or 12 leftover 1-1/2-inch biscuits

Preheat oven 450F (230C).

On a lightly floured surface, roll out dough to 1/2 inch thick. Using a 1-1/2-inch cutter dipped in flour, cut out biscuits. Place on an ungreased baking sheet. Bake 12 to 15 minutes or until golden; set aside to cool.

Berry Filling:

6 cups fresh or 2 (12-oz.) pkgs. frozen blackberries, boysenberries, loganberries or marionberries
1/2 cup granulated sugar
2 tablespoons quick-cooking tapioca
1 tablespoon lemon juice
1/2 cup orange juice, if using fresh berries
2 tablespoons melted butter or margarine

Preheat oven to 425F (220C). Grease a 10-inch-square baking pan or dish.

Gently wash fresh berries. In a large mixing bowl, carefully spoon together berries, sugar, tapioca, lemon juice and orange juice, if using fresh berries. Pour berry filling into greased baking pan or dish. Drizzle melted butter or margarine over berries. Bake 20 minutes.

Pain-Perdu Cobbler Batter:

4 eggs, well-beaten
1 cup half and half or 2% lowfat milk
2 teaspoons brandy or 1 teaspoon vanilla extract
3 tablespoons butter or margarine for frying

New Orleans-Style Topping:

Powdered sugar, ground cinnamon, ground nutmeg,
   lemon juice

Maple-Syrup Topping:

Pure maple syrup blended with whipped cream

In a large mixing bowl, whisk eggs, half and half or milk and brandy or vanilla until batter starts to foam. Soak biscuits in batter 2 to 3 minutes. In a large skillet over medium heat, melt 3 tablespoons butter or margarine. Cook biscuits to a light golden brown, about 1-1/2 minutes on each side. Drain on paper towels; then place on top of warm berry filling. Serve immediately New Orleans-style sprinkled with powdered sugar, cinnamon, nutmeg and lemon juice, or with maple syrup and whipped cream. Makes 6 or 7 servings.

Apple Cobbler Coffeecake

Instead of a large coffeecake, try serving this cinnamon-flavored apple cobbler for brunch.

Apple Filling:

**4-1/2 cups thinly sliced tart apples
   (6 medium-size apples)
1/4 cup chopped walnuts
1/2 cup granulated sugar
1/2 teaspoon ground cinnamon
1/2 cup raisins
2 tablespoons melted butter or margarine**

Preheat oven to 375F (190C). Grease a 9-inch-square baking pan or dish.

In a large mixing bowl, carefully spoon together apples, walnuts, sugar, cinnamon and raisins. Pour apple-walnut filling into greased baking pan or dish; drizzle melted butter or margarine on top and set aside.

Spiced Crisp Crust:

1-1/3 cups all-purpose flour
1/4 cup granulated sugar
1/4 cup packed brown sugar
1-1/2 teaspoons ground cinnamon
1/2 teaspoon ground mace
1/2 cup finely chopped walnuts
1/2 cup melted butter or margarine (1/4 lb.)
Vanilla Glaze, page 21, if desired

In another large mixing bowl, combine crust ingredients. Stir with a fork until dough is crumbly. Using your thumbs and fingertips, crumble dough on top of apple filling. Bake 30 to 35 minutes or until crust is crisp and golden brown. Cool 15 minutes before adding glaze, if desired. Makes 6 or 7 servings.

Meat & Poultry Cobblers

When serving a savory meat or poultry cobbler, crust options cover a wide range of possibilities. East Indian Lamb Cobbler is capped with a whole-wheat crust reminiscent of the breads often served with curry. Mouthwatering flavors of my hearty Sauerbraten Cobbler are captured under an intriguing gingersnap crust.

Pork & Prune Cobbler

A glazed poppy-seed and onion crust—made with buttermilk—tops a tasty pork and prune filling.

Pork & Prune Filling:

2 lbs. pork shoulder meat, cut into 1-1/2-inch cubes
2 tablespoons canola oil or safflower oil
1 garlic clove, minced
2 medium-size onions, thinly sliced
1-1/2 cups water
2 tablespoons soy sauce
2/3 cup white wine
1-1/2 teaspoons brown sugar
1 cup chopped pitted prunes

Grease a 9-inch-square baking pan or dish.

In a heavy skillet over medium heat, sauté pork in oil with garlic and sliced onions. When meat is brown, reduce heat to low and skim off fat. Stir in water, soy sauce, wine and brown sugar. Cover tightly and simmer 1 hour or until meat is tender. Add prunes and continue simmering another 15 minutes. Pour cooked pork filling into greased baking pan or dish; then set aside.

Buttermilk-Onion Crust:

1-1/2 cups all-purpose flour
2 teaspoons baking powder
1 teaspoon baking soda
2 teaspoons dried onion flakes
1/2 cup melted butter or margarine (1/4 lb.)
1/3 cup buttermilk
1 egg yolk
1 tablespoon buttermilk
1 teaspoon poppy seeds

Preheat oven to 425F (220C).

In a large mixing bowl, combine flour, baking powder, baking soda, onion flakes, melted butter or margarine and 1/3 cup buttermilk. Stir vigorously with a wooden spoon until a stiff dough forms. Spoon dough on top of pork filling to create a cobblestone effect. In a small bowl, whisk egg yolk, 1 tablespoon buttermilk and poppy seeds; then brush over dough. Bake 20 to 25 minutes or until crust is golden brown. Cool 5 minutes before serving. Makes 7 to 8 servings.

East Indian Lamb Cobbler

A spicy lamb stew combines perfectly with a whole-wheat biscuit crust.

Lamb Filling:

2-1/2 tablespoons olive oil

1-1/2 lbs. boned lamb shoulder,
   cut into 1-1/2-inch cubes

1/2 cup chopped onion (about 1 medium-size onion)

1 red bell pepper, chopped

2 teaspoons finely chopped fresh ginger root

2 garlic cloves, minced

1/2 cup water

Salt and pepper to taste

1/2 teaspoon ground cardamom

1/2 teaspoon ground allspice

1/2 teaspoon ground nutmeg

Pinch of ground cinnamon

2 tablespoons pine nuts or slivered almonds, toasted

2 tablespoons chopped fresh cilantro

Preheat oven to 325F (165C).

Heat olive oil in a large heavy skillet over medium-high heat; add lamb, onion, chopped red pepper, ginger root and garlic. Cook, stirring frequently, until lamb is brown, then reduce to simmer. Stir in 1/2 cup water, salt and pepper, spices and toasted nuts. Sprinkle with chopped cilantro. Pour lamb filling into a 9-inch baking dish. Cover tightly and bake 1 hour or until meat is tender. Carefully skim off fat.

Whole-Wheat Biscuit Crust:

3/4 cup all-purpose flour
1/4 cup whole-wheat flour
1-1/4 teaspoons baking powder
Pinch of salt
1/4 cup melted butter or margarine (4 tablespoons)
About 1/4 cup whole milk or 2% lowfat milk
Fresh mint sprigs and chopped red pepper, for garnish

In a large mixing bowl, combine flours, baking powder and salt. Gradually stir in melted butter or margarine and milk until dough clings together. On a lightly floured surface, gently roll out dough to fit baking dish. Carefully place dough on top of lamb filling. Cut a few slashes in dough so steam can escape. Increase oven temperature to 425F (220C) and bake 20 to 25 minutes or until crust is golden brown. Cool 5 minutes before serving. Garnish individual servings with mint sprigs and chopped red pepper. Pass around Yogurt Topping.

Yogurt Topping:

1-1/2 cups plain lowfat yogurt
1 garlic clove, minced
1 tablespoon chopped fresh mint

Just before serving, combine yogurt, garlic and mint in a small bowl. Makes 5 or 6 servings.

Sauerbraten Cobbler

A rich biscuit made with crumbled gingersnap cookies enhances the sweet and sour sauerbraten filling.

Sauerbraten Filling:

2 lbs. boneless beef chuck or rump roast,
  cut into 1-1/2-inch pieces
1 garlic clove, minced
Pinch of freshly ground black pepper
2 cups water
2 cups red wine vinegar
2 medium-size onions, chopped
1 teaspoon peppercorns
1 bay leaf
2 cloves
1/3 cup packed brown sugar
1 tablespoon all-purpose flour
2 tablespoons canola oil or safflower oil
1/3 cup tomato juice
Salt to taste
1/2 cup dairy sour cream

Grease a 9-inch-square baking pan or dish.

In a large bowl, combine meat, garlic and pepper. In a medium saucepan, bring water, vinegar, onions, peppercorns, bay leaf, cloves and sugar to a boil; stir until sugar has dissolved. Pour hot marinade over beef, cover and refrigerate at least 4 hours. Drain meat; strain and reserve marinade. Sprinkle flour over meat. In a large saucepan over medium heat, heat oil. Add meat and brown thoroughly. Stir in reserved marinade and bring to a boil. Cover and reduce heat to low; simmer 1-1/2 hours. Slowly stir tomato juice, salt and sour cream into meat. Pour filling into greased baking pan or dish.

Gingersnap Crust:

1 cup all-purpose flour
2 teaspoons baking powder
1/2 cup crumbled gingersnap cookies
1/4 cup melted butter or margarine (4 tablespoons)
1/2 cup whole milk or 2% lowfat milk
Dairy sour cream

Preheat oven to 425F (220C).

In a large mixing bowl, combine crust ingredients. Stir vigorously with a wooden spoon until a stiff dough forms. Spoon dough on top of sauerbraten filling to create a cobblestone effect. Bake 20 to 25 minutes or until crust is golden brown. Cool 10 minutes; then serve with sour cream. Makes 5 or 6 servings.

Beef-Bourguignon Cobbler

Using tender sirloin tips instead of stew meat saves on cooking time.

Beef-Bourguignon Filling:

1 tablespoon canola oil or safflower oil

2 lbs. (1/2-inch-thick) sirloin tip roast,
    cut into 1-inch pieces

1 (10-oz.) pkg. thawed frozen boiling onions

2 bacon slices, chopped

1/2 teaspoon salt

1 teaspoon chopped fresh marjoram or
    1/2 teaspoon dried-leaf marjoram

1/2 teaspoon chopped fresh thyme or
    1/4 teaspoon dried-leaf thyme

1 teaspoon black pepper

1-1/2 tablespoons all-purpose flour

1-1/2 cups beef broth

2 tablespoons tomato paste

1-1/2 cups red Burgundy wine

1 cup chopped mushrooms (1/4 lb. or 3 or 4 large)

Grease a 9-inch-square baking dish.

Heat oil in a large skillet over medium heat. Brown sirloin pieces with onions and bacon. Sprinkle meat with salt, marjoram, thyme and black pepper. In a small bowl, whisk flour into beef broth; then pour into skillet. Reduce heat to low; stir in tomato paste, Burgundy and mushrooms. Cover and simmer 40 minutes or until meat is tender, stirring occasionally. Pour bourguignon filling into greased baking dish.

Bacon & Onion Crust:

1-1/2 cups all-purpose flour
2 teaspoons baking powder
1 teaspoon dried onion flakes
3 slices cooked finely chopped bacon
1/4 cup melted butter or margarine (4 tablespoons)
1/2 cup whole milk or 2% lowfat milk

Preheat oven to 425F (220C).

In a large mixing bowl, combine crust ingredients. Stir vigorously with a wooden spoon until a stiff dough forms. Spoon dough on top of cooked bourguignon filling to create a cobblestone effect. Bake 20 to 25 minutes or until crust is golden brown. Cool 5 minutes before serving. Makes 5 or 6 servings.

Turkey-Breast Cobbler

Imagine the stars of a Thanksgiving dinner combined into one large dish—a turkey-breast filling with mushrooms, layered with a cornbread-and-sage crust and topped with warm cranberry sauce.

Turkey Filling:

1/2 cup half and half or 2% lowfat milk

2 tablespoons cornstarch

1/4 cup finely chopped shallots

**2 cups chopped mushrooms
  (1/2 lb. or 6 large mushrooms)**

3 celery stalks, sliced

1/2 cup dry white wine

1-1/2 cups turkey or chicken stock

2/3 cup melted butter or margarine

1-1/2 lbs. cooked turkey breast, cut into chunks

**1 teaspoon chopped fresh tarragon or
  1/2 teaspoon dried-leaf tarragon**

Salt and pepper to taste

Grease a 13" x 9" baking pan or dish.

In a small bowl, combine half and half or milk and cornstarch; set aside. In a large saucepan, cook shallots, mushrooms and celery in wine and stock about 15 minutes or until softened. Reduce heat; then add butter or margarine, cornstarch mixture, turkey, tarragon and salt and pepper. Cook until sauce thickens. Pour turkey filling into greased baking pan or dish; then set aside.

Sage Cornbread Crust:

1 cup all-purpose flour

1 cup yellow or white stone-ground cornmeal

2-1/2 teaspoons baking powder

2 tablespoons granulated sugar
2 teaspoons chopped fresh sage or
  1 teaspoon rubbed sage
Pinch of salt
1/4 cup melted butter or margarine (4 tablespoons)
1/2 cup whole milk or 2% lowfat milk
1 egg, well-beaten

Preheat oven to 400F (205C).

In a large mixing bowl, combine crust ingredients. Stir vigorously with a wooden spoon about 30 seconds or until a soft dough forms. Drop spoonfuls of dough over filling to create a cobblestone effect. Bake 30 to 35 minutes or until a toothpick inserted in center comes out clean. Cool 5 minutes before serving with Cranberry Sauce.

Cranberry Sauce:

1/2 cup cranberries
1/2 cup water
1/4 cup packed brown sugar
2 tablespoons lemon juice

While cornbread crust is baking, bring cranberries and water to a boil in a large saucepan. Reduce heat, cover and simmer 5 to 10 minutes or until cranberries are soft. Stir in brown sugar and lemon juice. Serve sauce warm. Makes 9 to 10 servings.

Chicken & Spinach Cobbler

Here's another consummate cobbler, a one-dish meal featuring a chicken and spinach filling with a herb biscuit crust.

Chicken-Spinach Filling:

1 lb. fresh spinach or 1 (10-oz.) pkg. thawed frozen
   cut spinach
2 lbs. boneless skinned chicken breasts
1 (10-oz.) pkg. thawed frozen boiling onions
1/2 teaspoon cornstarch
3 tablespoons lemon juice
   (juice of 1 medium-size lemon)
1/3 cup white wine
2 garlic cloves, minced
3 tablespoons grated Parmesan cheese
Salt and pepper to taste

Preheat oven to 350F (175C). Lightly grease a 9-inch-square baking pan or dish with olive oil.

Wash fresh spinach thoroughly; drain fresh or thawed frozen spinach well. Chop spinach. Cut chicken into 1-inch pieces. Place in lightly greased baking pan or dish with spinach and onions. In a small bowl, whisk cornstarch, lemon juice and white wine until blended. Pour mixture over chicken filling; stir in garlic, Parmesan cheese, salt and pepper. Bake 20 minutes; set aside.

Herbed Whole-Wheat Biscuit Crust:

1 cup all-purpose flour
1/4 cup whole-wheat flour
2 teaspoons baking powder
1 tablespoon chopped fresh parsley or
  1 teaspoon dried parsley flakes
1/4 teaspoon dried-leaf thyme
1/2 teaspoon dried rosemary
1/4 cup melted butter or margarine (4 tablespoons)
1/3 cup half and half or 2% lowfat milk

In a large mixing bowl, combine crust ingredients.
Stir vigorously with a wooden spoon until a stiff dough
forms. Spoon dough on top of chicken filling to create
a cobblestone effect. Increase heat to 425F (220C). Bake
20 to 25 minutes or until crust is golden brown. Cool 5
minutes before serving. Makes 4 or 5 servings.

Chicken-Dijon Cobbler

A simple biscuit crust combined with a classic filling from the ancient French province of Burgundy.

Chicken-Dijon Filling:

2 lbs. boneless skinned chicken breasts
1/4 cup butter or margarine (4 tablespoons)
2 garlic cloves, minced
2 tablespoons all-purpose flour
3/4 cup chicken broth
3/4 cup whipping cream or 2% lowfat milk
2 tablespoons Dijon-style mustard
Salt and pepper to taste
1/4 cup sliced pimiento-stuffed olives

Grease a 9-inch-square baking pan or dish.

Cut chicken into 1-inch pieces. In a large skillet, melt butter or margarine over medium heat. Add chicken and garlic; cook 5 to 10 minutes or until chicken is tender. Place chicken in greased baking pan or dish, reserving pan drippings. Over low heat, whisk flour and broth slowly into chicken drippings. Add cream or milk and continue to whisk until thickened; stir in mustard, salt and pepper. Pour sauce over chicken and sprinkle with sliced olives; then set aside.

Onion-Mustard Crust:

1-1/2 cups all-purpose flour
2 teaspoons baking powder
1/2 teaspoon dry mustard
2 teaspoons dried onion flakes
1/4 cup melted butter or margarine (4 tablespoons)
1/2 cup half and half or 2% lowfat milk

Preheat oven to 425F (220C).

In a large mixing bowl, combine crust ingredients. Stir vigorously with a wooden spoon about 30 seconds or until a stiff dough forms. Spoon dough on top of chicken filling to create a cobblestone effect. Bake 20 to 25 minutes or until crust is golden brown. Cool 5 minutes before serving. Makes 4 servings.

Chicken-Mornay Cobbler

This large cobbler features Mornay sauce, named after Philippe de Mornay, a French Huguenot gourmand. The sauce is made with equal quantities of Gruyère and grated Parmesan.

Chicken-Mornay Filling:

3 lbs. boneless skinned chicken breasts
1/4 cup butter or margarine (4 tablespoons)
1 garlic clove, minced
1-1/2 tablespoons chopped fresh or dried parsley
1 cup seedless grapes
2 tablespoons all-purpose flour
1-1/2 cups chicken broth
1/2 cup half and half or 2% lowfat milk
1/2 cup grated Gruyère cheese (2 oz.)
1/2 cup grated Parmesan cheese (2 oz.)
Salt and pepper to taste

Lightly grease a 13" x 9" baking pan or dish.

Cut chicken into 1-inch pieces. In a large skillet, melt butter or margarine over medium heat. Add chicken and garlic; cook 5 to 10 minutes or until chicken is tender. Place chicken in lightly greased baking pan or dish, reserving pan drippings. Sprinkle parsley and grapes over chicken. Over low heat, whisk flour and broth slowly into chicken drippings. Add half and half or milk and continue to whisk until thickened; slowly stir in Gruyère cheese, Parmesan cheese, salt and pepper. Pour sauce over chicken and set aside.

Garlic Crust:

2 cups all-purpose flour
2-1/2 teaspoons baking powder
1 teaspoon baking soda
1 teaspoon curry powder
1 garlic clove, minced
1 egg, well-beaten
1/4 cup melted butter or margarine (4 tablespoons)
2/3 cup buttermilk

Preheat oven to 425F (220C).

In a large mixing bowl, combine crust ingredients. Stir vigorously with a wooden spoon about 30 seconds or until a soft dough forms. Drop spoonfuls of dough on top of filling to create a cobblestone effect. Bake 20 to 25 minutes or until crust is golden brown. Cool 5 minutes before serving. Makes 9 to 10 servings.

African Meat Cobbler

A spicy beef and lamb cobbler with vegetables.

Meat & Vegetable Filling:

1-1/2 lbs. lean ground beef
1 lb. lean ground lamb
3/4 teaspoon ground coriander
1/2 teaspoon ground cinnamon
1 teaspoon black pepper
Salt to taste
1 bay leaf
3 medium-size carrots, shredded
3 medium-size zucchini, sliced
2 finely chopped scallions
1 large red bell pepper, chopped
3 tablespoons lemon juice
    (juice of 1 medium-size lemon)
2 tablespoons cornstarch
2 cups orange juice
1/4 cup peanuts
1/4 cup golden raisins

In a large skillet over medium heat, cook ground meat with coriander, cinnamon, black pepper, salt and bay leaf 30 minutes or until meat is tender. Add carrots, zucchini, scallions, red pepper and lemon juice. Cook 5 minutes or until tender. In a small bowl, blend cornstarch and 1/4 cup orange juice. Stir cornstarch mixture into meat mixture with remaining orange juice. Reduce heat and simmer until sauce has thickened. Stir in peanuts and golden raisins. Place meat filling in an ungreased 13" x 9" baking pan or dish.

Nutmeg Crust:

2 cups all-purpose flour
2-1/2 teaspoons baking powder
Pinch of salt
1/2 teaspoon ground nutmeg
1 egg, well-beaten
1/4 cup melted butter or margarine (4 tablespoons)
1/2 cup whole milk or 2% lowfat milk

Preheat oven to 425F (220C).

In a large mixing bowl, combine crust ingredients. Stir vigorously with a wooden spoon about 30 seconds or until a soft dough forms. Drop spoonfuls of dough on top of meat filling to create a cobblestone effect. Bake 20 to 25 minutes or until crust is golden brown. Cool 5 minutes before serving. Makes 7 or 8 servings.

Vegetable Cobblers

These colorful vegetable cobblers feature a variety of different crusts from the classic rolled to a mint-flavored cornbread. Enjoy them as vegetarian entrees or novel side dishes.

Chiles-Rellenos Cobbler

Here's an easy version of a classic Mexican recipe.

Chiles-Rellenos Filling:

3 eggs
1 cup half and half or 2% lowfat milk
3 tablespoons all-purpose flour
3 (4-oz.) cans whole green chiles, peeled
1 cup shredded sharp Cheddar cheese (4 oz.)
1/2 cup shredded Monterey Jack cheese (2 oz.)
1/2 teaspoon ground coriander

Preheat oven to 375F (190C). Grease an 8-inch square baking pan or dish.

In a large mixing bowl, beat eggs, half and half or milk and flour until smooth; set aside. Split open chiles and remove all seeds. In a large bowl, combine cheeses. Place chiles in greased baking pan or dish; then spoon about 2 heaping tablespoons mixed cheeses into each chile. Fold to enclose cheese. Sprinkle remaining cheese on top of chiles. Gently pour egg mixture over cheese-filled chiles; sprinkle with coriander. Bake 15 minutes.

Cornbread Crust:

3/4 cup all-purpose flour
3/4 cup yellow or white stone-ground cornmeal
2 teaspoons baking powder
2 tablespoons granulated sugar
1/4 teaspoon ground cilantro
Pinch of salt
1/4 cup melted butter or margarine (4 tablespoons)
1 egg, well-beaten
1/2 cup whole milk or 2% lowfat milk
Fresh tomato salsa and avocado slices

While filling is baking, start preparing crust. In a large mixing bowl, combine crust ingredients. Stir vigorously with a wooden spoon about 30 seconds or until a soft dough forms. When chile filling has baked 15 minutes, drop spoonfuls of cornbread dough over filling to create a cobblestone effect. Increase oven temperature to 400F (205C) and bake 30 to 35 minutes longer or until a toothpick inserted in center comes out clean. Cool 5 minutes before serving with fresh tomato salsa and avocado slices. Makes 7 to 8 servings.

Vegetable Cobbler

A hearty Mediterranean vegetable dish.

Vegetable Filling:

1/4 cup olive oil
1 medium-size onion, chopped
2 garlic cloves, minced
1 green bell pepper, chopped
1 red bell pepper, chopped
2 medium-size zucchini, sliced
1 summer squash, sliced
1 cup thawed frozen sliced carrots
1 cup thawed frozen broccoli flowerets
1/4 cup butter or margarine (4 tablespoons)
1/4 cup all-purpose flour
1 cup chicken broth
1 cup whole milk or 2% lowfat milk
1/2 teaspoon dried-leaf tarragon
1/2 teaspoon chopped fresh oregano or
  1/4 teaspoon dried-leaf oregano
Salt and pepper to taste

Grease a 10-inch-square baking dish.

In a large skillet, heat oil over medium heat. Add onion, garlic, bell peppers, zucchini and squash; sauté until softened. Add carrots and broccoli and sauté 2 to 3 minutes; set aside. In a large saucepan, melt butter or margarine over medium heat. Add flour and stir until mixture begins to foam. Gradually stir in chicken broth, milk, herbs, salt and pepper; continue stirring until mixture thickens and bubbles. Gently add vegetable mixture to sauce. Pour filling into greased baking dish; then set aside.

Rolled Cheddar Crust:

1 cup all-purpose flour
1-1/4 teaspoons baking powder
Pinch of salt
1/4 cup grated Cheddar cheese (1 oz.)
1/4 cup melted butter or margarine (4 tablespoons)
About 1/4 cup whole milk or 2% lowfat milk
1 egg yolk, slightly beaten
1 tablespoon whole milk or 2% lowfat milk

Sour cream mixed with chopped chives, if desired

6 oz. small-curd cottage cheese mixed with 1 teaspoon balsamic vinegar and some chopped chives, if desired

Preheat oven to 425F (220C).

In a large mixing bowl, combine flour, baking powder, salt and cheese. Gradually stir in melted butter or margarine and about 1/4 cup milk until dough clings together. On a lightly floured surface, gently roll out dough to fit baking pan or dish. Carefully place dough on top of vegetable filling. In a small bowl, whisk egg yolk and 1 tablespoon milk; then brush on top of crust Cut a few slashes in dough so steam can escape. Bake 20 to 25 minutes or until golden brown. Cool 10 minutes before serving with sour-cream or cottage-cheese mixture. Makes 5 or 6 servings.

Zucchini Cobbler

A colorful and spicy vegetable filling is topped with a mint-flavored cornbread crust to make a satisfying supper dish.

Zucchini Filling:

2 tablespoons olive oil
3 medium-size zucchini, thinly sliced
1 cup chopped mushrooms (1/4 lb. or 3 large)
1 large onion, chopped
1 cup drained whole-kernel corn
1/2 teaspoon turmeric
1/2 teaspoon ground coriander
2 garlic cloves, minced
1/4 cup chopped pimiento
1 tablespoon all-purpose flour
1/4 cup whole milk or 2% lowfat milk
3 eggs, slightly beaten
1 cup dairy sour cream
1 cup grated Swiss cheese (4 oz.)
Salt and pepper to taste

Grease an 8-inch-square baking pan or dish.

Heat oil in a large skillet over medium heat. Add zucchini, mushrooms and onion, sauté 4 to 5 minutes or until vegetables are soft. Reduce heat to low and add corn, turmeric, coriander and garlic, stirring frequently 10 to 15 minutes. Pour into greased baking pan or dish; sprinkle pimiento on top and set aside. In a large bowl, whisk flour, milk, eggs, sour cream, cheese, salt and pepper until blended. Pour mixture over top of vegetables and set aside.

Mint Cornbread Crust:

3/4 cup all-purpose flour

3/4 cup yellow or white stone-ground cornmeal

2 teaspoons baking powder

1 tablespoon granulated sugar

Pinch salt

1-1/2 tablespoons chopped fresh mint or
 1 tablespoon dried-leaf mint

1/4 cup melted butter or margarine (4 tablespoons)

1 egg, well-beaten

1/2 cup whole milk or 2% lowfat milk

Tomato chutney or relish

Preheat oven to 400F (205C).

In a large mixing bowl, combine crust ingredients. Stir vigorously with a wooden spoon until a soft dough forms. Drop spoonfuls of dough over vegetable filling to create a cobblestone effect. Bake 30 to 35 minutes or until a toothpick inserted in center comes out clean. Cool 5 minutes; then serve with tomato chutney or relish. Makes 5 or 6 servings.

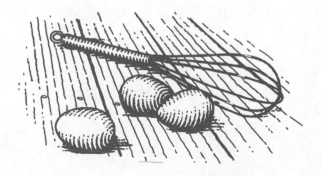

Caponata Cobbler

Caponata, a cold vegetable stew from Sicily, is transformed into a hearty main course when served warm and topped with an olive and Romano-flavored crust.

Marinara Sauce, page 100

Caponata Filling:

1 medium-size eggplant, peeled and cut into
   1/2-inch cubes
Salt
1/3 cup olive oil
1 medium-size onion, thinly sliced
1 garlic clove, minced
2 celery stalks, chopped
2 tablespoons capers
1/2 cup sliced pitted olives
1/4 cup red wine vinegar
2 tablespoons tomato paste
1 (15-oz.) can cut tomatoes
1 tablespoon maple syrup

Lightly grease a round 9-inch baking pan or dish.

Place eggplant cubes in a colander. Sprinkle with salt; then set aside to drain. In a large skillet, heat 1/2 of oil over medium heat. Add eggplant and sauté until lightly browned on all sides. Drain excess oil on paper towels. Sauté onion, garlic and celery in remaining olive oil 5 minutes. Add capers, olives, vinegar, tomato paste, cut tomatoes and maple syrup; cook 2 to 3 minutes. Pour into greased baking pan or dish; then set aside.

Olive-Romano Crust:

1-1/2 cups all-purpose flour
2 teaspoons baking powder
1 teaspoon baking soda
1 teaspoon granulated sugar
1 tablespoon grated Romano cheese
1/4 cup melted butter or margarine (4 tablespoons)
2/3 cup buttermilk
2 tablespoons pine nuts
1/4 cup sliced pitted olives

Preheat oven to 425F (225C).

In a large mixing bowl, combine crust ingredients. Stir vigorously with a wooden spoon until a soft dough forms. Spoon dough on top of caponata filling to create a cobblestone effect. Bake 20 to 25 minutes or until golden brown. Cool 5 minutes; then serve with Marinara Sauce. Makes 6 or 7 servings.

Fish & Seafood Cobblers

From New Orleans to the Maritime Coast comes a selection of Americana-inspired fish and seafood ideas for cobblers.

Fresh Crabmeat Cobbler

Fit for a celebration brunch or perfect for supper with a crisp green salad, this luxury cobbler is flavored with Madeira and lime.

Crab & Madeira Filling:

1/4 cup butter or margarine
1/4 cup all-purpose flour
1-1/2 cups half and half or 2% lowfat milk
3 tablespoons Madeira or dry sherry
2 tablespoons lime juice
2 tablespoons chopped chives
1 lb. cleaned, shelled, fresh crabmeat (3 cups)
1/2 cup thawed frozen tiny peas
1/4 teaspoon salt
1/4 teaspoon white pepper
Pinch of ground nutmeg

Preheat oven to 375F (190C). Grease an 8-inch-square baking dish.

In a medium saucepan, melt butter or margarine over medium heat. Add flour and stir until mixture begins to foam. Gradually stir in half and half or milk and continue stirring until mixture thickens and bubbles. Stir in remaining ingredients for filling. Pour into greased baking dish; then set aside.

Lime Crumb Topping:

3/4 cup all-purpose flour
1 teaspoon grated lime zest
1/2 teaspoon garlic powder
3 tablespoons melted butter or margarine

In a large mixing bowl, combine topping ingredients. Toss with a fork until crumbly. Using your thumbs and fingertips, crumble dough on top of crab filling. Bake 25 to 30 minutes or until crust is golden brown. Serve immediately. Makes 5 or 6 servings.

Herbed Fish Cobbler

Any firm white fish will work in this delicious supper cobbler.

Fish Filling:

2 lbs. firm white fish such as cod or halibut
Whole milk or 2% lowfat milk
1/4 cup butter or margarine (4 tablespoons)
1/4 cup all-purpose flour
2 teaspoons chopped capers
1/4 cup chopped fresh parsley
1/4 teaspoon dried dill
1/2 teaspoon mustard powder
1/4 teaspoon ground nutmeg
1-1/2 tablespoons lemon juice
Salt and pepper to taste

Grease a 9-inch-square baking dish.

Place fish in a medium saucepan; add enough milk to cover. Bring to a boil then reduce heat and simmer, covered, 5 to 10 minutes or until fish is barely done. Drain fish, reserving milk. Flake fish, removing and discarding skin and bones; set fish aside. Measure reserved milk and make up to 2 cups with additional milk if necessary. In a medium saucepan, melt butter or margarine over medium heat. Add flour and stir until mixture begins to foam. Gradually stir in reserved milk and continue stirring until mixture thickens and bubbles. Gently fold in flaked fish, capers, parsley, dill, mustard powder, nutmeg, lemon juice, salt and pepper. Pour into greased baking dish; then set aside.

Dill Buttermilk Biscuits:

1-1/2 cups all-purpose flour
1 teaspoon baking powder
1/2 teaspoon baking soda
1/4 teaspoon dried dill
1/4 teaspoon salt
1/4 cup melted butter or margarine (4 tablespoons)
1/3 cup buttermilk

Glaze:

1 egg
2 tablespoons water

Preheat oven to 425F (220C).

In a large mixing bowl, combine biscuit ingredients. Toss lightly with a fork until dough clings together. On a lightly floured surface, roll out dough to 1/2 inch thick. Using a 1-1/2-inch cutter dipped in flour, cut out about 12 biscuits. Arrange over fish filling. In a small bowl, beat egg with water; brush glaze over tops of biscuits. Bake 20 to 25 minutes or until biscuits are golden brown. Cool 10 minutes before serving. Makes 7 to 8 servings.

Seafood Gumbo Cobbler

*A classic gumbo filling combines perfectly with
cornbread biscuits for a superb one-dish meal.*

Gumbo Filling:

1/4 cup vegetable oil

1/4 cup all-purpose flour

1 cup clam juice

1 cup tomato juice

1/4 lb. crumbled cooked bacon

1 cup fresh okra, thinly sliced or
  1 (10-oz.) pkg. thawed frozen okra, thinly sliced

1 green bell pepper, chopped

1 green onion, chopped

1 clove garlic, minced

1 bay leaf

1/2 teaspoon freshly ground black pepper

2 tablespoons chopped fresh parsley

1 beefsteak tomato, seeded and diced

1/2 teaspoon paprika

1 teaspoon dried-leaf thyme

1 teaspoon dried-leaf oregano

1 teaspoon Worcestershire sauce

Dash of hot sauce

1/2 lb. small shrimp, peeled and deveined

1/2 lb. fresh crabmeat or firm white fish,
  cut into 1-inch pieces

3 tablespoons lemon juice
  (juice of 1 medium-sized lemon)

Lightly grease a 10-inch-square baking pan or dish.

In a large skillet, heat oil over medium heat; stir in flour.
Reduce heat, stirring constantly until flour mixture
(roux) darkens. Stir in clam juice and tomato juice until

blended. Gently stir in remaining filling ingredients except fish, shrimp and lemon juice; simmer, covered, about 30 minutes. Gently stir in shrimp, crab or fish, and lemon juice and cook 5 minutes longer. Pour gumbo filling into lightly greased baking pan or dish.

Cornbread Biscuits:

1/2 cup all-purpose flour
1 /2 cup yellow or white stone-ground cornmeal
1 teaspoon baking powder
1/2 teaspoon baking soda
1 teaspoon granulated sugar
Pinch of dried-leaf thyme
1/4 cup melted butter or margarine (4 tablespoons)
1 egg, well-beaten
2 tablespoons buttermilk

Preheat oven to 425F (220C).

In a large mixing bowl, combine biscuit ingredients. Toss lightly with a fork until dough clings together. On a lightly floured surface, roll out dough to 1/2 inch thick. Using a 1½-inch cutter dipped in flour, cut out about 9 biscuits. Arrange over gumbo filling. Bake 20 to 25 minutes or until biscuits are golden brown. Cool 5 minutes before serving. Makes 7 or 8 servings.

Salmon & Mushroom Cobbler

Canned salmon is dressed up in an herb-scented
mushroom sauce and topped with green-onion biscuits.

Salmon Filling:

1/2 cup butter or margarine
2 cups chopped mushrooms (1/2 lb. or 6 large)
2 tablespoons finely chopped shallots or green onions
1 teaspoon chopped fresh tarragon or
   1/2 teaspoon dried-leaf tarragon
1/2 teaspoon chopped fresh chervil or
   1/4 teaspoon dried-leaf chervil
1 tablespoon chopped fresh parsley or
   1 teaspoon dried parsley flakes
1/4 cup all-purpose flour
1-1/2 cups whole milk or 2% lowfat milk
1 tablespoon Dijon mustard
2 tablespoons white wine
2 tablespoons lemon juice
Salt and pepper to taste
1-1/2 (15-1/2-oz.) cans salmon, drained, boned
   and flaked

Grease a 9-inch-square baking dish.

In a medium skillet, melt 1/4 cup butter or margarine over medium heat. Add mushrooms, shallots or green onions and herbs. Sauté about 5 minutes or until softened; set aside. In a medium saucepan, melt 1/4 cup butter or margarine over medium heat. Add flour and stir until mixture begins to foam. Gradually stir in milk and continue stirring until mixture thickens and bubbles. Remove from heat and stir in mushroom mixture, mustard, white wine, lemon juice, salt and pepper.

With a fork, gently mix in salmon. Pour salmon filling into greased baking dish; then set aside.

Green-Onion Buttermilk Biscuits:

1-1/2 cups all-purpose flour
1 teaspoon baking powder
1/2 teaspoon baking soda
1/4 teaspoon salt
3 tablespoons finely chopped green onions
1/4 cup melted butter or margarine (4 tablespoons)
1/3 cup buttermilk

Glaze:

1 egg
2 tablespoons water

Preheat oven to 425F (220C).

In a large mixing bowl, combine biscuit ingredients. Toss lightly with a fork until dough clings together. On a lightly floured surface, roll out dough to 1/2 inch thick. Using a 1-1/2-inch cutter dipped in flour, cut out about 12 biscuits. Arrange over filling. In a small bowl, beat egg with water; brush glaze over tops of biscuits. Bake 20 to 25 minutes or until biscuits are golden brown. Cool 5 minutes before serving. Makes 6 or 7 servings.

Index